BIG M, little m Marketing

BIG M, little m Marketing

New Strategies for a New Asia

David Ketchum

John Wiley & Sons (Asia) Pte Ltd

Published by John Wiley & Sons (Asia) Pte Ltd
2 Clementi Loop, #02-01, Singapore 129809

Other Wiley Editorial Offices

John Wiley & Sons, Inc., 111 River Street, Hoboken, NJ 07030, USA
John Wiley & Sons Ltd, The Atrium, Southern Gate, Chichester PO19 8SQ, England
John Wiley & Sons (Canada) Ltd, 22 Worcester Road, Rexdale, Ontario M9W 1L1, Canada
John Wiley & Sons Australia Ltd, 33 Park Road (PO Box 1226), Milton, Queensland 4046, Australia
Wiley-VCH, Pappelallee 3, 69469 Weinheim, Germany

Library of Congress Cataloging-in-Publishing Data:
ISBN 0471-47923-3

Typeset in Times New Roman 11/13 by H. Beck
Printed in Singapore by Saik Wah Press Ltd
10 9 8 7 6 5 4 3 2 1

To my wife Jane,
and daughters Harriet and Emily,
to whom I said goodbye
and shut the study door for more
Sunday afternoons than I can count to get
this book from brain to page.

CONTENTS

Acknowledgments

With my tongue firmly in my cheek, I'd like to thank my co-author Google (www.google.com). Just about any topic typed into the search toolbar pops up instantly, and the website was a valuable tool for finding forgotten facts and discovering references. With a minimum of typing, I navigated from The University of Hawaii, to web pages filled with Japanese proverbs, to Fortune's "Asia Top 50" list, to the World Economic Forum, and the home pages of dozens of Asia-based and multinational companies. Having so much relevant information organized so clearly in such a short time helps make context clearer and draws connections across vast amounts of practical business source materials, as well as scholarly writing. Some of the most useful websites I visited are included in the Navigation Tools section.

This book is a compendium of what has interested me and proved useful in my business career in Asia. Therefore, much of the thanks for the contents (none of the blame) must go to the many, many colleagues, journalists and friends I've worked with since first coming to Asia in 1991. At the risk of leaving someone out, I'd like to particularly thank the following people for their ideas and encouragement throughout the process, which started with brainstorming the BIG M, little m Marketing concept and ended with the finished manuscript:

Paul Adams, Gregg Ainsworth, Geoffrey and Mary Barker, Mark Bobek, Tom Braithwaite, Farland Chang, Diana David, Paul Dien, Darby C. Doll, Dinda Elliott, Sarah Fraser, Cameron Honarvar, Conny Jamieson, Peter Kingsbury, Jean Liu, Paul Mottram, Whitney Small, Josephine Price, Louisa Wong Rousseau, Jake Statham, Hans Tung, Terri Tyminski, Helen Webby, and Frank Yu.

And also thanks to everyone at Wiley: Nick Wallwork who always accentuated the positive, Malar Manoharan for keeping one eye on the prose and one eye on the schedule, CJ Hwu and Grace Pundyk for their detailed and objective reading; Chris Newson and Adeline Lim for their help and support in marketing the book.

Preface

Although many international management theories and "how-to" business books deal with strategic planning and how to develop an integrated marketing campaign, until now there has not been a book that brings these ideas together in the context of the unique social and economic influences of Asia.

Yes, Asia really *is* different. Global learning is valuable, but we do need our own guide for navigation in our own region.

BIG M, little m Marketing: The Guide to Gaining Competitive Advantage in the new Asia is a view of the way forward for all businesspeople operating in Asia to unlock the marketing potential of what I believe will be a definitive era of rapid economic and social change. The reforms and liberalization that began with the aftermath of the 1997 financial crisis and that are gathering momentum with the coming of the WTO to China and Taiwan are just the beginning. This accelerating pace of change is now altering the face of the competitive landscape. The changes are inexorable. The nimble will be rewarded with new opportunities and profit potential, while the inflexible and moribund will face obliteration.

Chances are you are now standing in a bookstore. Sure, Amazon.com and other online booksellers now account for around 11% of all books sold in the US and a good chunk of the rest of the world market, but that just means there is a better than 89% chance you're in a bookstore. You've seen the alluring cover up there among all the other business books on the shelf, and you've taken it down. You're saying to yourself (or rather thinking, because it's a little weird to talk to yourself in public):

1) Can I skim this book right here and learn the gist of what it has to give me and then put it back on the shelf without buying it?

2) What on earth is *BIG M, little m Marketing* and why should I care after reading (or perhaps buying and then NOT reading) dozens of business books about "10 rules for this" or "revolutionary ideas about that"?

3) Is the marketing environment in Asia so different from the rest of the world that it needs its own book?

The answers to your questions are:

1) Yes, but I hope you get hooked;

2) BIG M, little m Marketing is a way to align your marketing strategies and tactics in a powerful combination for competitive advantage in Asia; and

3) Yes, Asia really *is* different. Global learning is valuable in to Asia, but we *do* need our own guide for navigation in our own region.

BIG M, little Marketing is not a textbook. It's not a "bible". It's not the Tao of Asian marketing. It's not a rulebook. It *is* an anecdotal guide – based on my own experience – and the dozens of companies referenced in the text – on how to make the most of the marketing opportunities in Asia to benefit your business and your own career.

I do hope you find BIG M, little m Marketing interesting and useful, and I welcome any and all comments, witticisms and criticisms you may wish to share at david@upstreamasia.com.
For updates and additional information, check out www.BIGMlittlem.com.

David Ketchum

Hong Kong, February 2003

1
Introduction

Right at the beginning I want to define what the term *Asia* refers to in this book: all markets from Japan to New Zealand, from India to Indonesia. This is the broadest definition possible. It encompasses the whole geography, and "Asian" does not refer to a racial distinction, but rather to anyone living or working in the region.

This book is built in large part on a paradox: even though Asia is changing perhaps more rapidly than any region in the world, its marketing practices all too often remain paralyzed by conservative business cultures resistant to innovation. Despite this, I believe that much of the secret of success in Asian business can be found by understanding its underlying stabilizing values and dynamics so as not to be pushed off by the vagaries of the "crisis of the day." A company's marketing edge may just as likely come from an MBA's theory as it does an ancient Asian proverb. And one of the aims of this book is to clearly articulate some ways to balance progressive, global best practice with respect for the deep-seated ways of doing business in the region.

I now run Upstream Asia, a marketing and communications consultancy with offices in Hong Kong, Singapore, Taipei and affiliates in China, Japan, Australia, and throughout the region. Previously, I was senior vice president of marketing and communications for Calvin Klein in Asia-Pacific, and before that was vice president of marketing services for global public relations firm Burson-Marsteller (initially for Greater China and later head of the Korea operation). In these roles I have seen the benefits of bringing together global best practice with local pragmatism, and worked with a wide range of locally-based companies and multinationals.

From this experience, the insights in this book came into focus slowly and steadily over the years, as I noticed consistent patterns across all aspects of marketing in the region. Whether in Japan or Singapore, or in fashion or technology marketing, I found many of the same dynamics at work. I have learned to harness these forces both to help our clients and to build our own business at Upstream Asia, and have pulled them together under the umbrella of BIG M, little m Marketing.

BIG M, little m Marketing: New Strategies for a New Asia is just like any other guidebook, except here the travel destinations are marketing ones such as achieving high public awareness of your company or product, gaining a compelling brand positioning, developing strong customer relationships, and sales success. Use it to find your way across the rapidly changing terrain of the marketing landscape in Asia. It doesn't have all the answers, but it does have tools and travelers' tales that will help you navigate your way to success. As with any other guidebook, please flip through it, skip sections, leave it on the shelf, loan it to friends, revisit it when you have a need, and draw your own conclusions about the content based on how relevant it is to your own experience.

The travel and navigation metaphors throughout the book serve as a unifying framework for the topics and chapters, which taken together lead the reader to an understanding of the power of BIG M, little m Marketing in Asia:

- **The Compass** – The BIG M, little m Marketing concept is the Compass that helps the marketer steer a straight course by understanding the fundamental role of strategy and tactics, and their relationship to one another. As with North and South, *strategy* (BIG M) and *tactics* (little m) are polar opposites of the same world, and an understanding where one is heading is essential for success.

- **The Map** – This section shows how to plot your location on the BIG M, little m Marketing Map, and understand where you have to head next to reach your destination. Just as the traveler can plot a course that is North-by-Northwest, so too the BIG M, little m Marketer can combine strategy and tactics in sophisticated ways to guide him or her unerringly. We will also explore the changing marketing topography in Asia today, and see what obstacles and opportunities await.

- **Eight Signposts to Success** – Chapter by chapter along the way, fwe discover principles for good marketing in Asia, illustrated with lots of examples. You may now wonder what these are, and soon you'll understand the meaning of:

  EAT THE ELEPHANT ONE BITE AT A TIME
  UNDER PROMISE AND OVER DELIVER
  EMBRACE YOUR WEAKNESSES
  THE VISION THING
  MOVE UPSTREAM
  GO, GO, GO!
  IT'S THE CUSTOMER, STUPID
  STEAL THE WHEEL!

- **Navigation Tools** – Now that you have your Compass, Map and Signposts, the final section of the book provides a compilation of tools, checklists, reference materials and ideas to help you reach your destination.

The companies and examples used come from many sources within top regional and international marketing-driven enterprises, as well as ad agencies and marketing consultancies. I also make reference to many of the companies with which I have worked directly. This is not done to promote these companies out of proportion with their market importance, but simply because these are the case studies I know best. (In the "Companies and Organizations" appendix at the end of this book I have identified by asterisk those companies where I worked or have been involved with, so any insider's perspective is revealed.) In order to avoid having the reader's flow interrupted by footnotes in the text, I have included all attributions and references for each chapter in the "Sources and Notes section at the end of the book."

Whether you work with an Asia-based company or a multinational company expanding into the region, you will find powerful marketing solutions that fit the specific Asian market conditions and customer demands in BIG M, little m Marketing. No matter who you are, if you can gain some competitive advantage for yourself or your business from BIG M, little m Marketing, then this book will have been a success.

BIG M,
little m
Marketing

"Lay plans for the accomplishment of the difficult before it becomes difficult; make something big by starting with it when small."

- Lao-tzu

2

BIG M, little m Marketing

BIG M, little m Marketing is a way of approaching marketing built around the central idea that if you can match the right strategy with the right tactics and implement the campaign well, all the other pieces will fall into place. It is particularly relevant to Asia because it has been my experience that most marketers in the region either confuse strategy with tactics or are unaware of strategy altogether, failing to see the big picture – BIG M – issues that are needed to drive the tactical details, the little m. All too often in Asia, tactical marketing initiatives are represented as strategies, whereas in fact the company actually has no strategy.

For most marketing problems, there are always at least several possible strategies that could be used as solutions, and there are literally hundreds of tactics that can be harnessed to implement the chosen strategy. Managers who spend time with their customers, carefully understand their needs, and understand their own company's strengths and weaknesses will be rewarded with successful marketing campaigns. Yet picking the right strategy is not enough if you cannot implement it properly. Being great at marketing tactics is of no use if you don't understand the big picture. Matching all the elements together is the hallmark of a successful BIG M, little m Marketing campaign, and is more relevant today in Asia than anywhere else in the world.

The Asian marketing environment since 1997 has been buffeted by shock waves of change, some pushed in from the global economy and some more local in their origins:

- 1997 — Asian financial crisis
- 1999-2000 — Internet Bubble
- September 2001 — World Trade Center attacks and aftermath
- December 2001 — China and Taiwan's accession to WTO
- 2002 — Accounting scandals and stock market slides

Much of what is old and proven will continue to work and be useful, but must be revisited, analyzed and put into a new context. The new marketing environment in Asia is coming into focus as part of an evolutionary process, but businesses' response must be nothing short of revolutionary. The problem is that business, by its very nature, is essentially conservative. Business is about identifying and managing ways to make money, and then vigorously protecting the *status quo* in order to assure a continued stream of revenue. Companies may add new products and services, and expand to additional markets, but the fundamental business dynamics remain the same.

This conservative track is particularly entrenched in Asia, where some companies have grown used to a minimum of competition, and in many cases close cooperation with government to ensure that the regulatory environment does not overburden business operations. Businesses rarely take revolutionary steps except when the main players in a sector are threatened by merger or are acquired, when immediate and new competing technology threatens, or when an industry is rapidly deregulated. The situation is compounded by the fact that marketing practice in the region has been impaired by the profession's inability to attract the best talent: historically many of the best candidates have been drawn into banking, property or management of local conglomerates.

Free and open competition is beginning to gain a foothold in Asia, and many businesses will be swept away because they have built what they believe to be solid, successful foundations on principles that will be kicked out from under them in the coming years. Established interests are digging in and resisting competition, such as some governments, entrenched family-owned businesses, and cartels. However, resistance is futile as the environment for marketing products and services undergoes fundamental changes. The pace of that change is set to accelerate, and the survivors must adapt their marketing starting now. The time is past for mere revision and updating of traditional marketing approaches in Asia; it is a time for all companies to take a revolutionary look at how they win, service, and keep their customers.

The impact of these changes will be felt for years to come, and although some locally based and international business people have seen some of the signs and even acknowledged some of the new forces at work, few have yet begun to truly revamp their strategies and practices to meet the challenges and new opportunities. The managers and owners of these businesses must either become alert to the new dynamics of the marketplace and change their business practices, or face consolidation or failure.

A recent market survey report, "Marketing in South East Asia", conducted by Singapore-based marketing consultancy High-Tech Associates, in conjunction with Ad Asia and The Chartered Institute of Marketing showed that many Asian businesses still lack an understanding of the importance of marketing as an integral part of their business success. Of the companies surveyed, 34% treat marketing on an ad hoc basis, without tying marketing expenditure to any tried and tested method, such as percent of turnover or gross profit.

Younger businesses that are just gaining momentum now – and which were perhaps completely unheard of five years ago – may well have the inside track to become the leaders of tomorrow. They have equal access to the tools of marketing strategy – and do not have the falsely comforting history of some of the more established players, nor the baggage of legacy IT systems and supply chains, and management thinking that may drag today's leaders down.

In the emerging, more openly competitive Asia marketing environment, many of the past "safety nets" that protected companies from losses – and which also served as barriers to younger companies wishing to push into a sector – are being removed. The clubby environment of government and business in collusion is breaking down in many Asian countries, and the process of awarding contracts, selecting distribution channels, and hiring staff has already become somewhat more transparent.

The opportunity for new competitors in a sector is now greater, but so too is the level of risk, because the margin for error in this newly, more competitive environment is becoming increasingly thin. For example, relationships are still powerful drivers of Asia business, but those companies that consistently come up with better strategic ideas and then implement them are increasingly earning competitive advantage.

Although not a complete transformation, these moves towards transparency and a leveling of the competitive playing field have put tremendous pressure on Asian business people to master the art of BIG M, little m Marketing. Strategy formulation and the selection and execution of appropriate tactics become increasingly important and also more difficult against the backdrop of change in Asia-Pacific marketplaces. Making BIG M, little m Marketing work for you is first about understanding the changes that are taking place and how they will affect your business. Second, you must compile the right, sustainable strategy and implement a compatible, realistic tactical marketing campaign.

So what are the forces that are tugging at the moorings of marketing in Asia? What are the local eddies and global undercurrents pushing the new Asia along on the tide? These trends and their impact will be examined in more detail throughout the rest of this book, but here is an overview of the forces reshaping the Asia business landscape.

Small reforms and innovations will tip the balance among established players, entrepreneurs, and multinationals in the region. The outward changes to the competitive scene may be barely visible, but the introduction of subtle yet innovative new technologies, trading regulations, and political and social changes will be the basis of tomorrow's competitive advantage.

The impact of ***globalization*** is being deepened and sped up by the fact that many countries in Asia are former colonies of Western nations (with Thailand as the notable exception) or have otherwise developed interdependencies with international economies. Many economies in the region naturally leapfrog several technological stages of development, as in the case of countries such as Vietnam, which has more mobile telephone subscribers than "plain old telephone service" landline users. Whether this is accomplished by having the vision to swiftly adopt the best technology and best practice – for example Malaysia – or just a historical accident, the end result is that the forces of globalization are now rapidly driving the business agenda.

Simultaneously, ***nationalism*** provides a massive and productive counter force to globalization, as nations and markets strive to achieve a better-than-global standard to protect the market share of their own goods in their own markets, and to drive overseas expansion. For example, HSBC, the Hong Kong-spawned but London-based bank, has energetically grown itself into a world player in the last decade.

Relationships have always been seen as essential to Asia business. Now, however, new relationships are as likely to be based on price, contacts made via the Internet, and vendors offering superior service and marketing, as they are to be on old-fashioned connections of family, religion or nationalism. Although these so-called "bamboo networks" are still powerful forces in Asia, they may be knocked aside on a case-by-case basis where there is a clear economic advantage to doing things differently.

Cultural differences are increasingly swept away by the profit motive, and age-old trading communities such as the *hua' ch'iao* (overseas Chinese) are being joined by ***new communities based on shared economic interest and combined buying power***.

Companies in Asia will ***adopt global "best-practice" management only where it makes sense, and ignore it when it is not applicable to the local context***. To date, many business managers in Asia have been distracted and misguided by slavishly following business trends from the US and Europe that may not fit their needs.

Newspapers, magazines, TV, radio, and websites are changing from being locally controlled mouthpieces for domestic political and economic agendas, to ***more free and open sources of consumer and political information***, viewpoints, and contacts. This shift is in part pushed along by freedom of the press, and also by the economic necessity of creating content that is both relevant and revenue generating.

As companies worldwide are discovering, ***interactions with customers are conversations***, not one-way broadcasts. Today's customer is expecting a personalized dialogue in his/her relationship with a company or brand and the Asia region is set to be the scene of some of the most important customer/business interactions anywhere in the world. Emerging customer relationship management (CRM) technology automates and simplifies some of the processes involved, but interpersonal relationships are never going to be replaced.

Many of the old players will evolve and thrive, but their future success will be based on ***solid marketing strategies***. Today, in lieu of marketing strategies, many companies still simply sell their products at an attractive price point, relying on volume growth at any margin and the "pile 'em high and sell 'em cheap" mentality to build and sustain market share. As a product reaches the end of its life cycle, it is simply dropped from the line, rather than being re-positioned or re-invigorated.

The current era in Asian business is dominated by distribution, as manufacturers and marketers *PUSH* goods out into sales channels. ***The next era will harness the power of PULL***, with marketers meeting demand for what customers want, when they want it, where they want it, and at what price.

These major power shifts and trends will drive Asia marketing for many years to come. Is this list comprehensive? No. Set in stone? No. Is it entirely new and unanticipated? Also no. However, these factors taken all together serve as a loud wake-up call for companies who do not have their BIG M, little m Marketing strategies in place.

Inside the Asia business community, companies are gathering resources to meet the new challenges. But management tools such as global best practices and entrepreneurial innovation that will challenge the old order of business, are developing slowly and are not always relevant to what's happening in the region. What businesses the world over are realizing – and which will be confronted perhaps most forcefully, and occasionally most painfully, in Asia - is that coming to terms with the new market conditions requires a jump shift in mindset.

Table 1
CHANGING ASPIRATIONS AND OBJECTIVES
A World of Change in the Asian Marketing Environment

OLD	NEW
International empire building	Developing truly global business
Business based on existing relationships	New relationships based on business
Collusion and deals to ensure distribution and sales	Market share earned via superior marketing
Local, insular, protectionist marketplace	More open international competition
Parrot-like adoption of international trends	Filtering what works best in Asia
Entrenched businesses dominate	The best run businesses dominate
Vertically intergrated "command and control"	Outsourcing and supply chain management
Large scale = economies and power	Specific/Customised = relevant and viable
The media is a tool for information control	Debate about freedom of the press is on the agenda
Family/government relationships	Customer relationships
Customers are "acquired" and talked at	Customers are engaged in conversation
Tactical, sales driven activities	Strategic, marketing-driven campaigns
Manufacture and PUSH	Understanding customer demand and PULL
Reliance on *guanxi* (connections) and the status quo	Leverage existing business practise, but improve it

Some businesses will wait for a cataclysmic event to compel them to first understand, and then react to, the inexorable, massive changes that have occurred around them. Others will resist change, and some will perhaps continue to be successful if they can hold on to their established interests. None, however, will be unaffected. *BIG M, little m Marketing* is a guide for both companies and individuals to take control and create their own revolutionary path forward within this context, without waiting for outside forces to compel them to change. *BIG, M little m Marketing* is both a mindset and a set of tools for competitive advantage; broken down into its strategies and tactical counterparts. *BIG M, little m Marketing* is not a virgin theory that just appeared out of nowhere. Instead, it is a fresh and radical recombination of winning elements into a way of looking at marketing and thinking about business in Asia that is intended to jolt businesses awake before they are swept away by crisis.

Across Asia, the pace of change will be faster in some places, and slower in others. However, businesses everywhere will find themselves forced into categories that will determine their fate:

Existing companies, that

- are forced to change by the changing marketplace and successfully evolve;
- are confronted by unexpected change and fail;
- anticipate change and re-organize for competitive advantage;
- anticipate change but choose the wrong path.

New enterprises, that

- spot market opportunity in change and successfully meet specific customer needs;
- jump into new business niches and are crushed by existing companies.

Whatever category your company falls into or hopes to fall into, *BIG M, little m Marketing* provides a powerful framework for analyzing your market position and setting the right course of action for business success.

The next chapter looks at the cultural and economic forces that have made the practice of marketing in Asia what it is today, as a backdrop to the rapid changes the coming era will require.

Asian Sense and Business Sensibility

"Asia is modernizing in 'the Asia way'."

- John Naisbitt

"Even underwear has national characteristics."

- John Bryan, CEO of Sara Lee Corporation, commenting on global marketing

3

Asian Sense and Business Sensibility

This is a book about change, and about opportunities for competitive advantage in Asia. In order to anticipate the force of these changes, and implications for what is possible in marketing, the underlying cultural influences on the way business is done in the region must be understood. For those who are natives or who have lived and worked in Asia for many years, this chapter may give you a new perspective on what you already know. For those who are new to the region, these insights into the cultural context of marketing in the region are useful in effectively applying the principles of BIG M, little m Marketing.

Anyone who has spent any time in Asia, whether living and working "in country" or dashing through the five-star hotel lobbies of Shanghai or Kuala Lumpur on the way to the airport, is familiar with the clichés of doing business in the region, such as:

- Relationships matter.
- Gift-giving is important.
- Giving your partner "face" is as much a part of the transaction as the price paid or service provided.
- Asian companies tend to be very hierarchical, with only senior executives granted decision-making powers.

One of the reasons these have become clichés is because they are often true, and many generations of international business people seeking to swiftly understand the dynamics of what are actually very complex interactions turn to the same simple formulas to get results.

Probing behind the clichés, however, reveals some insights into why the professional practice of marketing in Asia has not advanced far, and helps illuminate what is and is not possible for BIG M and little m Marketing. Behaviors can change, but values seldom if ever do.

There is such a diversity of cultures, economic development, role of government, and social structures of markets across Asia that it is difficult to make sweeping generalizations about the region. There are, however, a number of deep-rooted constants that have significant and ongoing influences on many of the everyday business transactions in the region.

Confucianism

Confucianism's deep influence on the dynamics of marketing across many Asian nationalities and cultures is not just historical, it is current and vital. The fact that the family unit is regarded as the source of social stability and political order has contributed to the formation of powerful trading networks across the region. The principles of Confucianism define an individual's identity in the context of one's family or group, and that has economic implications for how people relate to companies and brands. Belief in the value of hard work and self-improvement in a collective effort to achieve group results can be a powerful force for successful implementation of BIG M Marketing strategies.

Within organizations, the importance of elders as respected leaders and clear hierarchies can help drive both BIG M and little m Marketing initiatives forward in ways that perhaps a Western business culture focused on the importance and rewarding of the individual might not allow. The collectivist tenets of Confucianism have also contributed to the strength of many of the dominant business entities in the region, such as the Japanese *keiretsu*, and the Korean *chaebol* groups of companies.

Another influence of Confucianism on marketing in Asia is the fact that the role of "merchant" or business person is not defined in the otherwise clear and ordered definition of the roles of people in society. Confucianism defines the hierarchy of many relationships: ruler to minister, father to son, husband to wife, elder brother to younger brother, and friend to friend. However, the relationships of merchant to customer, buyer to seller, and all other commercial interactions go undefined, and historically have not been particularly valued. In the Confucian view, merchants are strangers with a profit motive, and not to be trusted.

As durable as the Confucian worldview has been through the centuries, it does not prepare society for the increasingly intrusive role of business in people's lives. The complexities of modern commerce, such as anonymous transactions over the Internet, or free market competition, were certainly originally unforeseen. A central challenge to the development of BIG M Marketing in the region, as elsewhere in the world, has been to work out how to make the strange familiar (unknown products and services, people, brands, and companies), and to build business relationships and trust with companies and brands within the existing mindset.

As the daily impact of Confucianism on people's lives becomes less pervasive, company executives and marketing professionals are being freed to integrate marketing approaches brought in from other cultures, and increasingly Western "best practice" is creeping into the Asian marketer's thinking. The smart BIG M, little m Marketer knows how to harness best practice, without turning his or her back on the strengths and traditions of the existing ways of doing business. Some local practices may be less efficient than new ways of doing things, but the fact that they have been working for centuries can often be reason enough to include them in the new marketing plan.

Tracing the Chinese Networks

Just about everywhere in Asia (except Japan) there are centuries-old networks of traders and merchants of Chinese descent. The common race, family interconnections, and shared culture have helped guide the way business is conducted across the region and has profoundly influenced the role of marketing strategy and tactics in commerce. The overseas Chinese are by no means the only trading network, but the so-called *hua-ch'iao*, has been a lasting engine of commerce in markets as widespread as Malaysia and India, as well as Greater China.

The overseas Chinese have a heritage of widespread immigration, and the preservation of a racially and culturally homogenous trading community internationally is part of the network's continued success. This network of family ties and relationships is still at the root of many of the region's major supply chains from raw materials to manufacturing to wholesaling and retail sales. This vertical continuity throughout the supply chain has short-circuited many of the dynamics of free market economies, in which buyer and seller negotiate, and price and demand are set by market factors. In a free market, two parties often negotiate but can't reach agreement based on price or terms of business. Conversely, in racially and culturally cohesive trading communities such as the overseas Chinese, business people have a strong incentive to reach a mutually satisfactory conclusion, and to keep the transaction within that community. Sometimes the terms might not be as favorable as what could be negotiated in open market negotiations, and sometimes they are even better.

This practice can be seen in action at Hutchison Whampoa and the other companies associated with Li Ka-shing, the shipping, property and telecom tycoon, and Hong Kong's richest man. The Group encompasses a trading empire that directly or indirectly controls 16% of the market capitalization of the Hong Kong Stock market. The associated companies trade extensively among themselves. They are housed and pay rent in buildings constructed and owned by Cheung Kong Holdings, Mr Li's flagship property company. Hutchison Whampoa handles construction and building maintenance. Employees use Orange mobile telephone service, shop at Park 'n Shop and Watson's, and the list goes on and on.

This networking provides a significant base of business for group companies to operate from, and reduces the importance of marketing strategy. Having a group of potential customers who are pre-disposed to do business with you whatever your products or services are, and whatever the price or customer service level is means there is little need to develop in-depth marketing strategies – the business just comes in and goes out. This little m-driven approach can be highly efficient, and also can lead to some business deals that are convenient though perhaps not particularly strategic. For example, Hutchison gained 700 new retail outlets in the U.K. with its purchase of the superdrug mass-market chain and then announced plans to expand its 3G-phone service sales network via superdrug. Some analysts queried whether low-end superdrug was the right retail environment in which to reach 3G's high-end prospective customers. The unstated answer is that although the BIG M strategy may not be 100% right, the little m efficiencies of driving one of the company's products through another of its distribution channels is irresistible.

When a company is part of a powerful conglomerate, the parent handles many of the usual BIG M Marketing functions such as brand positioning and establishing distribution systems. Such companies have ready-made opportunities to push their products and services into established distribution channels at good margins, so they generally only need to focus on little m Marketing. The marketing director's task is straightforward: to run various product and promotional initiatives that target existing customers and a group of clearly understood, accessible prospective customers.

Although the network of Li Ka-shing-aligned enterprises is indicative of the way Asia trading communities work – and many similar examples can be found in Japan, Malaysia, Indonesia, and elsewhere – it is not a purely Chinese model. Li Ka-shing and Hutchison owe a strong debt of heritage to the British colonial institution of the *hongs* (or trading houses, such as Swire and Jardine Matheson) that have dominated Hong Kong's trading existence from the earliest days of commerce.

The overseas Chinese network also facilitates marketing in Asia because of the cultural consistency and cohesive belief system that has allowed large groups of people to develop a common business understanding. Merchants of Chinese descent share many of the same values and understanding of what constitutes accepted practice. Although sharing a bond, they trace their heritages back to many provinces and many cities, and speak a wide range of dialects from Hokkien to Cantonese. As Lynn Pan says in *Sons of the Yellow Emperor*, "The theory that all Chinese are ultimately descended from a common ancestor rests on the tradition that the Yellow Emperor had 25 sons, 14 of whom were given distinct surnames by their father. A consciousness of shared origin no doubt compensated for the feeling of being lost in a new country."

It is true that throughout many centuries, the various clans of the *hua-ch'iao* have competed fiercely against one another, and there *are* differences among the Chinese subcultures. However, despite these differences, the Chinese overseas share a belief in China's special place in the cosmos as the Middle Kingdom between heaven and earth. These Chinese overseas have been bonded together by common cultural and economic interests. These ties have helped create a relatively efficient and harmonious economic environment in which the participants are predisposed to do business with one another. In this environment, the focus is not on developing customer driven BIG M Marketing strategies, but rather on the little m Marketing aspects of making deals and driving business with others in the trading community. In the new, emerging marketing environment, the power of these comfortable, established networks would come under threat as companies are increasingly incentivized to work with those companies that offer the best service and the most added value, rather than simply the strongest relationship.

Putting Marketing in Context

Communications and marketing are inextricably linked. Marketing has been defined as "communicating messages with an intended business result." The communications style for most Asian cultures is what is called "high context," and this orientation has a profound influence on how people communicate with one another, and on the practice of marketing.

For effective communications to happen between two people, a key question is how much background knowledge (or context) can be assumed? How much information does an individual have to be provided with before he or she gets the right message? In high-context cultures, people require a complete understanding of the situation before they are able to effectively communicate. In this mode, the status of the person delivering the message can be as much a part of the communications process as the meaning of the message itself.

A simple but dramatic example of this comes from McDonald's in China. When the restaurant chain was first rolling out in China, they did just about everything according to the internationally successful template. That included the introduction of the Ronald McDonald clown character, both in advertising and in their promotions. McDonald's has a training program for clowns, and at considerable expense, Chinese Ronalds were selected and sent to the US for training as the company's ambassadors. A problem: Chinese children had no exposure to clowns and had no idea what they were or what they represented. At opening time, the massive, grinning, oddly dressed figures did not inspire visions of fun and frivolity, but rather were terrifying to some young customers. Without the contextual meaning of what a clown represents, the meaning was lost and perhaps even potentially harmful to business. But for some reason, the inanimate statues of Ronald seated on benches were a hit, especially for families taking photographs. Marketing messages that are simply crisp and blunt in a low-context culture can be indecipherable or offensive in high-context cultures.

Another example is the young executive who was helping out with the sponsorship of the Johnnie Walker Classic golf tournament in Thailand one year. This sports marketing campaign effectively reaches consumers, journalists and restaurant and bar operators, and works well to position the brand. His boss asked him to make sure that each journalist covering the golf tournament that day be offered a gift bottle of whisky, and he replied that he had enough bottles for everyone. At the very last minute, as a double check on a hunch, the boss asked the employee if he had made sure to get Johnnie Walker Black Label. The employee recoiled, and said that no, he had not bought Johnnie Walker, but instead had selected a local Thai whisky brand because it was cheaper. At first glance, it was sheer stupidity of the employee to not make the connection between the sponsor's product and the gift to the journalists, but at another level the boss was careful enough not to assume too much in a high-context society in which sports marketing was just getting started.

Businesses in Asia often focus on detailed, tactical marketing because they have had to carefully control the context, tone, and intent of their marketing messages to precisely target their potential consumers. The bulk of the marketing effort in high-context cultures is placed on building a relationship with the customer (adding more and more context), rather than "blasting out" messages that will be seen by many, but have relevance for few. In Asian marketing today, when a message is delivered, it is often spelled out with more objective persuasion, logic, and clear-cut conclusions than in the West.

In addition to being high context, many Asian cultures are also "high ritual." The ways people interact with one another are bound by tradition and/or strictly defined rules of behavior. Historically, marketers in Asia have focused on marketing tactics, because they had cultural and commercial incentives to conform and promote their goods and services in ways that are acceptable and proven, if not particularly daring. As is the case worldwide to greater and lesser degrees, business people in Asia try to minimize commercial risk and any threats to their livelihood. It's easy to understand why many business people would not want to pursue an innovative BIG M strategy that might risk offending or baffling customers, especially if a proven little m tactical approach yields sustained sales and profits. For example, it would be hard to imagine advertising along the lines of the controversial Benetton AIDS campaign originating in Asia.

Relationships

Setting aside all the clichés about the importance of relationships in marketing in Asia cultures, the fact remains that global marketers can learn a lot about customer relationship-building from the Asian example. The whole world is moving from command and control BIG M marketing strategies to approaches which rely more and more on relationship marketing and viral marketing techniques. Increasingly, marketing is being regarded as an interactive process in a social context. This trend is born out by the tremendous success Internet marketers have had with viral marketing on the Web, such as Hotmail which is free for all and where every mail has a message at the bottom offering the service free to others. Other examples are the continued growth of Amway, Nu-Skin and other network marketers.

Conscientiously building relationships is certainly not unique to the Chinese, but they have honed the practice into a fine art. Whereas Western business people may expect a series of transactions to generate a relationship, the Chinese seek to build a successful track record of trustworthy interaction, and then believe the transactions will follow. Mainstream Western marketing practice has consistently advocated a *relationship* marketing approach for key customers, and a *transactional* approach for the less significant ones. In other words, make friends and build connections with your biggest customers, while simply supplying your product or service to your smaller customer in return for payment.

The practical truism is that in China just about every business interaction (whether local to local, or multinational) runs on relationships. The gift of a bottle of fine Cognac brandy to business associates has become such a commoditized sign of commitment to the relationship that in some parts of China, there are bottles of Cognac that have been given and "re-given" so many times their labels are wearing off. But more important than the act of gift giving is in understanding how these relationships in Asia affect the practice of the "4 Ps" (price, promotion, place, packaging), the guiding marketing principles generally accepted in the West. They still apply, but just like any tool for competitive advantage, they can be knocked aside by a better customer relationship. It is usual practice for Chinese firms to start by analyzing the strength of their relationships, and then determine how to maximize their use of them for business development.

Due to the pervasiveness of Confucianism, this same dynamic is apparent across the region. Foreigners arriving to do business in South Korea may receive a brutally frank but useful lesson from their new colleagues when they arrive in the country. Many an expatriate has discovered that nobody in the mainstream business community would be interested in doing business with them or their multinational company unless they brought along a significant technological advantage, investment dollars, or store of intellectual capital. This is because Korean executives have traditionally tended to evaluate potential partners based on what city they came from, which family they belonged to, which university they attended, and then later, for which company they worked. This mindset is a real obstacle for the international business person, because nothing in the foreigner's personal profile rates any points on the scale – even if they went to excellent international schools that are recognized in Korea, or worked for prestigious companies overseas; they just don't fit the Korean checklist for business social standing.

Although many surface-level aspects of Korean business culture have been transformed in the aftermath of the 1997 economic crisis and growing foreign ownership stakes in Korean business, much of the same dynamic still exists. This relationship-driven business climate is not conducive to BIG M Marketing, because if the relationship is critical to a business deal, then no objective research data or creative marketing concept can gain acceptance without the endorsement of a "gatekeeper" inside the culture who is willing to sponsor and endorse the idea.

Carefully cultivated customer relationships need to be maintained at both the wholesale, business-to-business level, and driven right down to the end user consumer level. Just as many Koreans believe that the origins and reputation of potential business partners are more significant than the business propositions they bring, so too with consumers, brand loyalty among Asians is powerful, and consumers will buy at retailers with "honored reputations." In economies where relationships are sacred, tremendous amounts of time, training and experience are needed in the marketing and sales departments. A Big M Marketing strategy in Asia is just as likely to be about customer service as it is about offering innovative products or bargain prices.

An indication of this level of service is the elaborate ritual that accompanies the opening of Japanese department stores in the morning, with all employees singing the company song, and providing a special greeting and thank you for the first customers of the day. However, this focus is changing, for although retailers' reputations and customer relationships are valued, they are no longer "silver bullets" in the winning and retention of customers, as evidenced by the recent wave of openings of discount stores across Japan. Japanese brands such as the popular Uni-Qlo clothing brand (selling inexpensive clothes made in China) and international players such as the hypermarket discount chain Carrefour are now making dramatic inroads to the retail sector.

Marketing Management Decision-Making

One of the hallmarks of BIG M, little m Marketing is that insight must be matched with decisive action. The fundamental business decisions that are made early on about what level of cost and quality will be offered to the customer can be the cornerstone of ongoing success – if the initial strategic impetus is followed through with a strong and sustained marketing campaign to make the business plan a reality.

The early and astounding success of Pohang Iron and Steel Company (Posco) in Korea illustrates the high dividends that can be realized when BIG M bravado is matched with military-style execution of little m tactics. Brigadier General Park Tae Joon, who was charged by the president of Korea, Park Chung Hee, to make good on the rallying cry "Steel is national power," started Posco. The Korean steel industry had failed to make any headway in the country's first five-year plan. Instead of targeting organic growth, Park Tae Joon treated the development of Posco like a military campaign, relying on Japanese financial support and technology to provide steel for Korea's burgeoning shipbuilding and automotive industries, and for export.

The heavy investment in capital expenditure on plants and IT infrastructure rapidly built the company that became the world's number seven steel producer. The price and quality equation of the Posco product met customer demand domestically and from all over the world, but the success of the company was by no means assured in the highly competitive global steel market. The forceful paramilitary execution of President Park's vision and Brigadier General Park's battle plan was at the heart of the success of the enterprise.

The development of BIG M, little m Marketing in Asia has been simultaneously helped and hurt by such traditional management structures that govern many corporations in the region. These clear-cut, hierarchical management structures concentrate authority with powerful executives who have the wherewithal to implement their vision and insight. On the one hand, this top management "command and control" environment is in some ways conducive to the success of BIG M, little m Marketing, and certainly has been demonstrated effectively at such corporations as Sony, where the leadership has had both the vision and the authority to execute.

On the other hand, a challenge to BIG M, little m Marketing in Asia is that strategic business information is sometimes too closely held by individuals in senior management, since it is often gathered through personal relationships from reliable sources. Gathering data and market insights in this way is cost effective, timely and reliable, and since it is proprietary to one company or even one individual, it can help keep competitors out or hamper their chances of success. The challenge is that the source of the data (and therefore its validity) is not as transparent to the company as it would be if (for example) it came from Procter & Gamble's research department. Additionally, since knowledge is power, the information may not be shared throughout the organisation with those who can make most effective business use of it.

When information is not shared with junior colleagues who may have more specialized skills or insights relating to their business unit, problems can arise. Sometimes crucial information is held by the manager who is most *entitled* to make a decision (thanks to his or her executive position), but whom is actually least *qualified* to make use of the competitive advantage the strategic marketing information offers. With a large "power distance" between senior management and more junior executives, those with new insights or differing points of view may not wish to seem disloyal, and may choose to take management's direction rather than upset a secure, harmonious situation. This behavior can block innovation and hamper efforts to do BIG M, little m Marketing.

Conversely, in a reverse twist on power distance, problems can also arise in cultures and companies (such as is sometimes the case in the Korea *chaebol* conglomerate companies) in which junior people formulate most of the solutions and decisions and then bring them to senior management for sign-off. The senior executives may be unaware of all the facts or context, and simply wait until their teams have done all the legwork and reached consensus on a particular decision. Management in these situations sometimes inadvertently validates weak or incorrect strategies due to the ceremonial aspects of their role in endorsing directions and policies already agreed on at a lower level.

There is an inherent contradiction in a business culture that both stresses consultative decision-making, and at the same time the absolute authority of the senior decision maker. The implication for BIG M, little m Marketing (particularly in large companies) has been that there can be a profound disconnect between management's BIG M Marketing vision and the little m Marketing activities. Perhaps their nimble decision making is one reason SMEs have flourished throughout the region – and contributed much marketing innovation. The best BIG M, little m Marketing companies minimize potential disconnects between management and workers (and vision and action).

Tupperware is an example of a company operating in Asia that has successfully harmonized BIG M and little m Marketing with its direct-selling business model. It has built a strong business internationally (only 20% of its sales are in the US) and in Asia by unlocking the entrepreneurial power of its individual "distributors." Freed from the constraints of traditional corporate hierarchies and business relationships, and empowered to make profits, the distributors can make far more money than they would in the confines of a traditional corporation. The worldwide business model has been brought in lock, stock, and barrel to the Asia region, with just a few adjustments to the product mix. In India, Tupperware has created special products to meet customers' needs, such as the sealable "Spice-it-up" container for jam and pickles. The direct selling method is matched with other more traditional local retail distribution and marketing methods, creating new opportunities both inside the established rigid business hierarchies, and by breaking out of them.

Another obstacle to Big M, little m Marketing is that many managers in Asia are culturally attuned to be "problem accepters," or "situation accepters," and accept fate as a significant variable in managing. An Asia-Pacific marketer may be more likely than his or her Western counterpart to look for a solution based on a past success, rather than a future solution. On the other hand, one of Asian management's tremendous strengths for Big M, little m Marketing is the collective decision-making process of many organisations. Although it may take longer for management to reach agreement on the strategic approach than in a Western context, once the team has made a decision, it will have a solid, stable consensus about the chosen direction that is unlikely to change in the face of adversity during implementation.

The savvy BIG M, little m Marketer will look past the differences between marketing practice in Asia and global best practice, and instead will focus on how to leverage the cultural strengths that help get business done efficiently. The myriad situational combinations of culture, context, relationships, economics, and trends are too dynamic and complex to summarize. Particularly when markets are being deregulated or are in flux, the wisest approach can be to ignore all the cultural sensitivities and relationships, and simply jump to the BIG M strategy that is best for the customer.

The ways deep-seated business cultures and trading habits influence marketing in Asia that we have looked at in this chapter may be rooted in centuries of tradition and culture, but they are not monolithic. Now, some but by no means a majority of the time-honored ways of doing business in the region are becoming less relevant or even completely swept aside. The hierarchical rigidity and cronyism that have typified much marketing and distribution in the region to date is particularly under pressure to reform. The groundswell of change is opening up new potential for business people to release tremendous marketing power.

Some of these changes are evident now, such as the impact of the Internet and China and Taiwan's accession to the WTO, but others are subtler. It is not as simple as saying: "The old ways of doing business will be cast aside and international principles will take hold." In fact, as we race into this period of dramatic change, we must continue to take into account the context of what is going on here in the region. This is not the United States of Asia or the Economic Union of the Pacific. We cannot assume that the latest marketing and management theories from the US and Europe have complete relevance and usefulness in this part of the world, and we need our own perspective on how to gain competitive advantage from the changes that lay ahead. And that is what the rest of this book will explore.

The COMPASS

An unerring sense of direction from
BIG M, little m Marketing

"In the beginner's mind there are many possibilities, but in the expert's mind there are few."

\- Shunryu Suzuki

4
The COMPASS

When you set out on a journey a Compass is one of the most useful aids you can have. Navigators have for centuries relied on having an unerring sense of where true north was, and for the marketer the equivalent is having a clear and compelling strategy to guide the business. Like north and south, BIG M strategy and little m tactics are polar opposites, but are also two directions on a single axis. The marketing strategy should indicate the tactical direction in the same way that if you know which way is north, then you know which direction is south. BIG M, little m Marketing is your Compass for determining your marketing course of action and staying on track.

Here's a working definition of BIG M, little m Marketing:

"The art of integrating 'BIG M' Marketing strategies with the appropriate well-executed'little m' Marketing tactics to efficiently and effectively gain competitive advantage."

The concept is universal; however, this book focuses on the specific relevance of BIG M, little m Marketing to Asia.

The three main attributes of BIG M, little m Marketing are:

The "BIG M" – strategy – is essential to any marketing or business plan, and is distinct from the tactical initiatives needed to implement it. For example: "Let's make a special 50% off offer" is a tactic. "Let's commit to giving consumers the lowest possible prices, and then make up what we lose by having low profit margins by building a high volume business" is a strategy.

The "little m" – tactics – is where the promise of the strategy is actually delivered. Tactics are often derided by marketing experts as mundane and to be taken for granted, but when they are properly targeted and executed, tactics drive business results. A consistent tactical campaign adhering to a clear, single-minded strategy can sustain a company for decades.

Bringing BIG M and little m Marketing together – Integration – is key to making the right strategy align with the right tactics and vice-versa. Integration is also a critical aspect of integrated marketing, in which a range of tactics all works together to help achieve the goals of a single strategy. Let's look at each aspect of the definition in more detail:

The Art

As with any human endeavor, there are real personal and cultural factors that affect marketing plans. For example, if the chairman of the board has a passion for golf and can't help meddling with the marketing plans, the company may sponsor golf tournaments, even if consumer research indicates that tennis is a better fit, or that the target audience rarely watches sporting events. Although this book aims to guide the marketer along the BIG M, little m path, if great marketing could truly be reduced to a formula, then everyone would do it equally well, and the competitive playing field would be leveled again. The reality is that BIG M, little m Marketing is more of an art than a science, and every marketer must find his or her own way using the tools provided.

Marketing

There are almost as many definitions of marketing as there are marketing executives, so rather than get bogged down in the details, let's jump to a time-honored-if-not-perfect definition:

"Marketing is the process of identifying and anticipating customer needs and meeting them, profitably."

Let's look more deeply at the components of the marketing process:

Identifying and anticipating customer needs ... Study your target customer's habits, personal requirements and desires and understand what drives them to the desired action (such as eating at your restaurant, visiting your website, buying your product).

Identifying customer needs is a fundamental BIG M Marketing function. Needs can be identified using an orderly process, such as extensive consumer testing, analysis of demographics and psychographics, and focus groups. Alternatively, especially for SMEs the process can be entirely personal and anecdotal. If a grocer notices that a particular brand of moon cake sells particularly well at Chinese New Year, and the next year at the same time orders in a bigger order of the same brand to meet his customers' anticipated needs, then that's just as valid as the scientific approach. At a more sophisticated level, insightful research and analysis is combined with a considerable amount of intuition and luck to help marketers anticipate what the customer desires.

... and meeting them ... This is the little m. Successfully and consistently delivering products or services over time that meet the target customer's need is more difficult than most businesses initially anticipate. Marketing campaigns sometimes fail *spectacularly* due to inadvertent mistakes, such as the "win a million pesos" Pepsi-Cola promotion in the Philippines in which thousands of cans had tabs with the winning number printed on them. More often than not, however, marketing fails *unspectacularly.* For example, a company may see its sales fall because a competitor prices a product just a few percent less, or comes up with a service that offers slightly better value for money.

...profitably... This is where the dreamers are separated from the true business people. Starting an airline that can fly from Singapore to London for US$200 is hard; doing it profitably is virtually impossible. There is absolutely no point in having a visionary strategy if it can't be executed, or having a wonderful BIG M dream if executing the little m details costs more than the revenue brought in.

Strategy

One definition of strategy is "a coherent marketing direction," which certainly fits with the Compass analogy for BIG M, little m Marketing. This definition provides some useful guidelines for formulating strategies. Strategies must hold together and represent a clear, unified approach. They also must provide direction – a roadmap for future action. Another, simpler definition of strategy is "a clever plan." Just formulating a plan is not strategic; it has to have a smart twist or a unique angle.

Tactics

Tactics are the activities used to fulfill the promise of the strategy. Most marketing is about creating the right environment to create sales. Tactics can be as simple as bringing the product "within arm's reach of desire" (Coca-Cola's distribution mantra) or as sophisticated as changing potential customers' perceptions so they are more likely to act (make a purchase). Advertising, promotions, public relations, special events, online marketing, and direct marketing are all examples of tactics.

The importance of effective execution of a tactical plan is underestimated by most marketing theorists. Perhaps the clearest thinking on the subject comes from authors Al Ries and Jack Trout in their 1989 book *Bottom-Up Marketing*, in which they argued that the most successful way to build a marketing strategy is to start at the bottom, and look for a tactic you can exploit. By starting with an effective tactic (a "competitive mental angle") and then building that tactic into a powerful strategy, you end up with a more coherent marketing direction than if you had started with an abstract strategic concept.

Integration

A lot has been written about integrated marketing, which is simply using tools from the many marketing disciplines together in a coordinated way. Integration in the context of BIG M, little m Marketing is different: it's about integrating the strategy with the tactics. Some marketing thinkers believe tactics should drive strategies; others believe in "top-down" planning, in which the strategy is determined and then the tactics are put in place. In fact, it really doesn't matter how it comes together, as long as it does come together, the one complementing the other. Integration is an iterative process rather than a straight line from problem to solution.

The ideal company and the savvy executive will have the vision to link marketing strategy with the tactics that support it. In reality, some companies are proficient at developing strategies. Others have excellent tactical execution. Some are smart enough or lucky enough to have both. Some companies operating in Asia have brilliant strategies they can't execute. Others have no strategy, but have built solid businesses anyway, due to luck, contacts, or the sheer will of the company's management to succeed.

Today in Asia, frequently the bigger questions of market competitiveness and distribution advantage are resolved in smoke-filled rooms by family or government-controlled organizations that short-circuit many of the usual free market checks and balances. When one company or cartel completely controls the means of distribution and pricing, the importance of BIG M Marketing is diminished. However, as noted in the introduction, this "little m" lock on marketing and distribution in Asia is progressively being broken, and the savvy marketer will need to rely more and more on the BIG M, little m Marketing Compass for guidance.

The BIG M, little m Marketing concept takes a broad and deep view of what marketing is. For example, a marketing director who realizes that his or her company has the wrong products to meet their customers' needs, and works with the design and operations departments to revamp the product offering is engaged in BIG M Marketing. Similarly, a strategic decision to change distribution channels can be BIG M Marketing. Any time that executives devise plans or make changes that bring the product or service more in line with customer demand, or that create a better environment for sales, can be considered BIG M Marketing.

The BIG M, little m Marketing Compass should be consulted frequently during the journey to customer satisfaction. Every customer interaction can drive the marketing campaign forward, but may also push the business a little bit off course, and continuous references to true north are needed to stay on track. As you work with the BIG M, little m Marketing concept more and more, you will find BIG M and little m references start to appear in your business conversations. Here are some ways the Compass can help keep you oriented:

- "Yes, the idea of offering discounts is a good one as far as the little m Marketing goes, but we still haven't tackled the BIG M issue of how we differentiate ourselves from our competitors."

- "The overall BIG M strategy has already been decided by our headquarters, and so the objective of this meeting is to brainstorm the little m tactics that will fulfill the global objectives."

- "This company has the right BIG M strategy, but without the right local partner they won't get anywhere in this market."

- "The entire little m Marketing activity plan needs to be thrown out since the company has repositioned itself to focus on business-to-business (B2B) customers."

- "The management consultants have identified the importance of marketing to the success of the merger. Now what's needed is a BIG M Marketing plan to convince the shareholders of the viability of the combined business."

As you start using BIG M, little m Marketing ideas in your marketing planning, you will find the concept grows in richness and usefulness. It is more than simply an answer to the questions, "Is this a strategy or is this a tactic?" and "Is this macro or is it micro marketing?" It embodies the beliefs that the two are different, yet inseparable, that strategy is fundamental to creating effective tactics, and that without well-executed tactics the most visionary strategy will not work.

The next chapter looks at how the BIG M and little m Marketing concepts can be used to create a Map of where you are, and where you want to get to.

The MAP

The lay of the land

"A blind man riding a blind horse reaches a deep pool at midnight."

- Chinese proverb

5

The MAP

The image of a blind man riding a blind horse at midnight sums up succinctly what is bad about much of the marketing that is done in Asia. Many companies in the region can't see where they are going, have nothing to guide them, and are headed for disaster. Some firms have both the BIG M and the little m aspects of their marketing wrong. Others have good strategies or good tactics, but not both.

For the marketing traveler, after the Compass, the Map is one of the most useful tools. The BIG M, little m Marketing Map can help plot where companies fall in terms of strategies and tactics, and provides an overview of where they need to move for future success. In the same way that cartographic maps are aligned by the points of the Compass (north, south, east and west), so too the BIG M, little m Marketing Map captures all possible combinations of a company's ability to use strategy and tactics: great strategy, weak tactics; great tactics, weak strategy; everything weak; and everything great. The BIG M, little m Marketing Map also indicates where companies need to move for future success.

On the Map and throughout this book, we'll plot in which quadrant a business lies, and the steps it needs to take to become "Mm Winners" – where BIG M and little m Marketing align.

Here's what you will find in each of the four quadrants:

- Companies in the upper left-hand of Quadrant One are the **"Dreamers",** companies that reach for great strategies and initially miss on the tactics. Many go on to revise and focus their BIG M, little m Marketing and become successful. These companies usually have more vision than business traction, and have often Charted out ambitious mission statements that they are not able to fulfill.

- Quadrant Two in the upper right-hand corner contains the **"Mm Winners"** that bring together the right marketing strategies with great tactical execution. They are the heroes of this book, because they have both developed compelling strategies, and tactically executed their plans to a very high standard.

- The **"Doers"** in Quadrant Four in the lower right-hand corner are companies that may be lacking in marketing strategy, but they plow dutifully ahead just the same. They either borrow other companies' strategies or focus single-mindedly on the tactical little m aspects of marketing and sometimes succeed in spite of themselves through sheer persistence and lucky market timing. However, their longer-term viability is at risk without an overarching strategy.

- The **"Duds"** languish in the lower left-hand of Quadrant Three. "Duds" have neither effective strategies nor the ability to execute properly, and the commercial viability of businesses in this quadrant is dubious. They are either headed for bankruptcy, or are supported by forces that keep them from failing, such as governments or family-controlled conglomerates.

The classification of businesses into one or another of the four quadrant categories reveals how companies should and should not use marketing strategies and tactics for success.

ILLUSTRATION 1. BIG M, little m Marketing Map

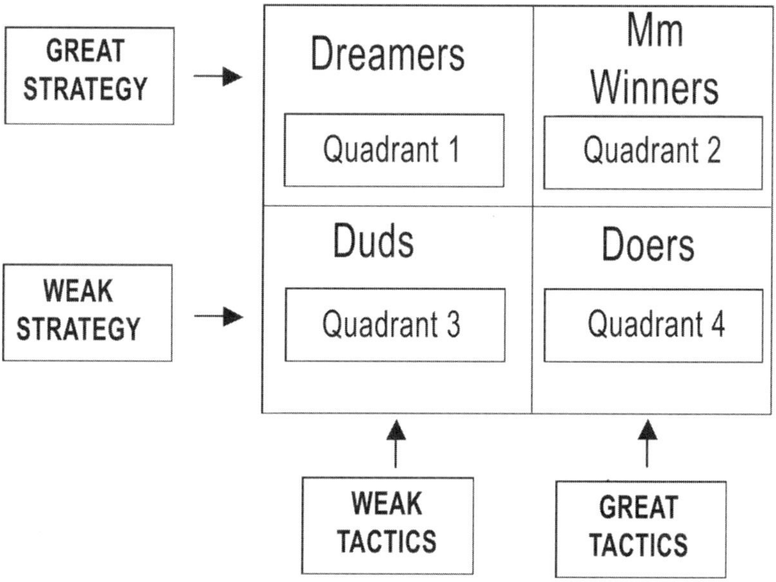

As with any map, some points are in between the four main quadrants. Just as a traveler can be heading north-by-northwest, so too a company can plot its marketing position precisely on the known coordinates of the Map.

In addition to their place within the overall Map, companies can also be plotted where they fall within each quadrant, and in which direction they are moving.

Where is your company or division on this Map? Are you an "Mm Winner?" And which way are you moving? Are you headed in the right direction? And if you are in the wrong quadrant, or heading the wrong way, how do you get back on track? The real insight for the marketer is not to be found in simply identifying what quadrant you are in. Instead, focus on which direction you are heading in, and at what speed. For example, the savvy manager and marketing executive can take a "Dud" company and address the BIG M, little m Marketing issues head on, and tap into tremendous hidden shareholder value and profit potential.

There are some diagnostic and navigation tools and resources to help you formulate strategies and tactics at the end of this book.

By looking at vignettes of Asia companies at work, we'll draw out the lessons that can be learned from firms in all four quadrants. As we map the positions of Dreamers, Mm Winners, Doers and Duds, we'll take a look at twelve hypothetical companies called "A" through "L" that are scattered all over the BIG M, little m Marketing Map and are moving in different directions at varying rates of speed. Look for the company that most closely resembles your own, and draw out the lessons learned and action steps required to take you to the next level.

Dreamers

"Dreamers" are the brilliant strategists who capture a clear vision of the way forward. Some "Dreamers" are able to successfully implement their vision, but others cannot bring to bear the tactics needed to bring their strategies to fruition. There are many successful companies in the "Dreamers" quadrant, but some here have little traction in the marketplace, or any long-term future. These companies could be multinationals that have the right "playbook," but are unable to execute their global strategies in Asia because they don't have the local contacts or partners to execute their visions; or companies that stubbornly implement global strategies without regard for local conditions. Other times Dreamers are local companies driven by savvy executives who can't execute well on their vision or who get caught out by market changes that leave them bankrupt.

"Dreamers" are sometimes successful and sometimes not, but they always have a clear BIG M Marketing vision of where the market is going and what their customers want. The achilles heel of Dreamers is their inability to execute practical, effective tactics against their strategies.

Many "pure play" Internet businesses from the dotcom bubble fell into this category. Their founders and their bankers initially had the right strategy and the vision, but either market circumstances conspired against them, or they were unable to gain any meaningful market presence before they ran out of money and went out of business. For example, in Hong Kong in 1999, Jimmy Lai's ADMart Web-based grocery and electronics home-delivery service showed potential. The Internet seemed poised to change the way commerce was done, the venture was well funded, and Lai is known as a daring and charismatic businessman with a proven track record in "old" media that people believed he could carry over to the Internet. In this context, ADMart seemed to have everything going for it, except of course a sufficient base of customers and revenue. At the height of the "experiment" the business was said to be losing US$10 million per month. ADMart was eventually closed when losses mounted and no buyer for the business was on the horizon. Jimmy Lai turned his attentions back to old media, including a successful drive into the Taiwanese market with his "Next" media properties.

Some Dreamers are overoptimistic about what resources are needed to make a product launch or marketing initiative successful. Other Dreamers do eventually match their vision with the right "on-the-ground" operations. A company may be in the Dreamer category but be sufficiently good at tactical implementation to be a viable business, approaching the border of the "Mm Winner" quadrant.

ILLUSTRATION 2. Dreamers on the Move

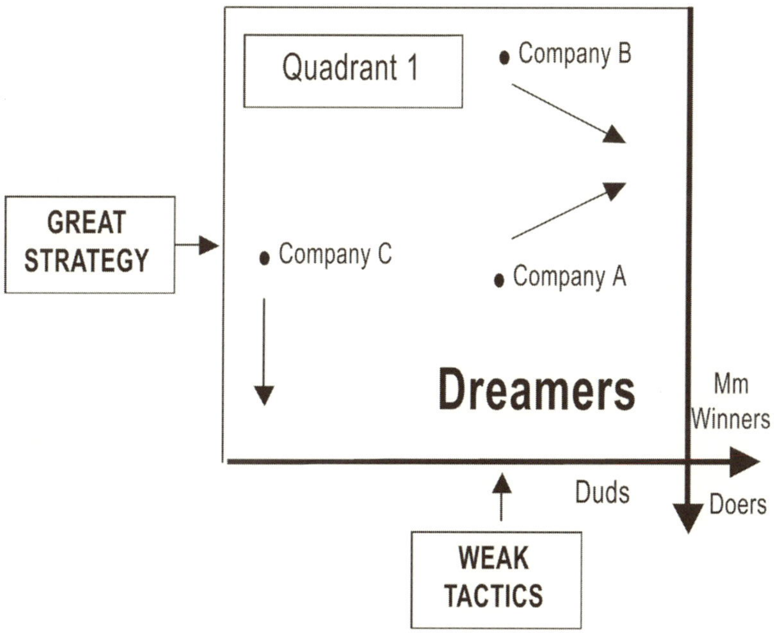

Where are you?

If your plotting puts you in Quadrant 1 of the Map, beware! It can be the right place to be if you have a powerful strategy and are working on getting the tactical execution right, but it can be a high-risk position if your vision gets ahead of what you are actually able to implement.

You could be in terrific shape with a clear BIG M vision of where your company is going and what you need to do. Sure, your little m tactics are not as effective as they could be, but you just put your new strategy in place last quarter, and it does take time for new marketing campaigns to start to show an effect, and for your marketing team to settle in to the new way of doing things.

On this Map of hypothetical Dreamers, we'll look at companies A, B, and C, which are all in Quadrant One, and they are all in motion.

Is your company like A: getting more proficient at strategy and tactics, and headed toward being an Mm Winner? Perhaps Company A just completed a long merger and integration process, and is now starting to build both strategic and tactical momentum as a combined company. In the example in Illustration 2, of all the companies, A seems to be the one heading in the right direction.

On the other hand, you don't want to be Company B: weak on tactics, and rapidly dropping out of the great strategy quadrant to become a Dud. Company B could be a firm that had visionary ideas but lost many of its core operations people to a competitor and is losing its tactical abilities. Company B, like Company A, is heading toward being a "Mm Winner" but seems to be losing proficiency in strategy at the same time. Maybe Company B has a new CEO with more vision and leadership abilities than the previous one, but who is less proficient at the operational details.

Company C has every chance of being a "Dud" in the near future if management does not slow the deterioration of its BIG M strategic direction. This company appears to be in the process of failing as strategists, and at the same time they are weak on execution. Immediate action is probably needed in the form of new management, an aggressive new strategy, or the intrusion of the board of directors to help determine the cause of the simultaneous BIG M, little m Marketing woes and fix them.

It's also worth looking at the velocity of the changes taking place. If a company is rapidly heading into another quadrant, it may be too late to act effectively. On the other hand, steady incremental change can be a useful monitoring tool for management to increase budgets, make new hires, change advertising agencies or calibrate any of the hundreds of variables that determine a company's marketing performance. And, if its moving too slowly in the chosen direction, then that can also be a danger signal that management is not moving fast enough, or acting decisively enough to make a real change in the company's position.

Being in Quadrant 1 is not a bad place to be for a short while, but the best "Dreamers" are the ones who use their time here as a milestone on the way to being an Mm Winner. Dreamers find it hard to maintain long-term viability and profitability unless their tactical abilities catch up with their strategies.

Dreamers in Action

This section looks at some instances in which companies have been stronger at strategy than execution, or have mismatched their BIG M and little m Marketing. Some of these examples are of specific projects in which vision exceeded execution, and many of these companies have gone on to be Mm Winners. These companies all faced the prospect of BIG M belly flops until they came to understand the marketing environment in which they were operating, and to match the right BIG M and little m Marketing campaign elements.

Slip Sliding Away

DuPont's efforts to make Teflon brand coating a success in China illustrate the value of adjusting BIG M strategies to line up with local little m realities to yield results, even if it means adopting ways of doing business that had never before been used elsewhere in the world. DuPont's marketing efforts in China went far beyond an analysis of customers' habits and cookware needs, and eventually led to a new way to make the product available to customers.

Use of DuPont's Teflon on cooking utensils in China got off to a slow start. Traditional wok cooking is a hot, hot metal-on-metal experience, with part of the culinary magic coming from the conjunction of high temperature oil, bare metal cooking implements and the scraping, turning use of a metal spatula. This cooking environment is not an immediately obvious place for a coating of Teflon, and early efforts to coat cookware in China resulted in consumers inadvertently scrapping the coating off woks and pans during the energetic cooking process. DuPont has been called a "guzinta" company, because it is an industry leader in creating and selling many other products including Teflon that "goes into" another company's product for the end user. DuPont's BIG M Marketing strategy in China followed the same template the company used successfully in the rest of the world: they licensed the use of Teflon brand coating to Chinese cookware manufacturers.

Some of DuPont's early B2B cookware manufacturing customers became dismayed by the consumer's experience with the product, and did not see the potential of using Teflon. Six years of trying to sell local pots and pans makers on the idea of using Teflon coating did not produce either the desired marketshare (they gained 80% of China's non-stick segment, but only 2% of the total domestic cookware market) or satisfactory business results. When DuPont decided to radically change its BIG M Marketing strategy, and for the first time anywhere, launched its own line of Teflon coated cookware, the company began to tap into the potential of the China market. DuPont rolled out the product with consumer education on the benefits and proper use of Teflon coated cookware, and built a brand that is now successfully distributed and sold throughout China.

DuPont's experience demonstrates how relentless focus on the business objective can drive a project to success, whereas a tactically oriented company in the same situation would have become lost. With the BIG M strategy of becoming the market leader in providing cooking utensil coatings firmly in mind, DuPont was able to step completely outside the boundaries of failing little m tactics to re-orient the entire approach to the market to meet the objective. No amount of revisions to the little m tactics would have ever achieved the results of re-inventing the whole market entry strategy.

Shots and Lenses

Also in China, a major multinational pharmaceutical company used its worldwide experience to set up a scheme to sell vaccinations through health insurance channels. The BIG M Marketing approach of appealing to consumers when they were thinking about health, and when an insurer would cover part of the expense, seemed to be as relevant to China as anywhere else. However (despite the success of the insurance industry in China), many Chinese consumers believe that it is bad luck to take out insurance because it pre-supposes that problems will occur, thus the drive to market the vaccine through this channel was not successful. Similarly, a global contact-lense manufacturer tried to implement its BIG M strategy of selling prescription lenses through ophthalmologists, only to find out that in China contact lenses can be bought over the counter with little checking of eye health. They then went on to build a sizable business using sales and distribution tactics that fit better with the local "over the counter" contact lens market.

Citroën is not a Lemon

The Taiwan operators of French car brand Citroën had a momentary "last mile" misfire in their BIG M, little m Marketing with a mix up in their copywriting. Citroën has some clear differentiating product characteristics, such as a pioneering hydro-pneumatic suspension to give superior ride, characterful ergonomics, and solid design and engineering. Taiwan, an easy fishing ground for the US players (with the advantages of US brand saliency due to US-Taiwan ties, and same side steering), has also proved attractive to European manufacturers.

In the early 1990s, Citroën was trying to establish its brand in Taiwan. France as the "country of origin" already had good equity due to the immense popularity of Cognac brandy in Taiwan, and it appeared that Citroën had a strong performance-related territory to own, namely the low air-resistance offered by its flagship XM. Co-efficient of drag (or "CD") had first been actively marketed as a feature on mass-produced cars in the early 1980s when Ford of Europe touted the "CD" of its then groundbreaking Sierra. Streamlining may seem irrelevant in Taipei, one of Asia's most traffic congested cities, but it was a true point of difference, and like all good positionings, potentially "ownable" by the brand. All the elements were in place for BIG M Marketing success in Taiwan.

So far so good. But the final link in the chain to little m Marketing snapped by what one can only guess was the result of a Chinese advertising copywriter working on a brief provided by a Frenchman. When the advertising broke, it made much of the XM's "excellent wind-breaking qualities," which instantly undid so much of the BIG M Marketing work that had gone before.

Cola Wars Go to China

These "last mile" BIG M, little m Marketing disconnects can happen to any marketer, as these cola war examples from China from two of the world's best marketers show. Pepsi's "Come alive with the Pepsi Generation" slogan was first inadvertently translated into Chinese to literally mean "Pepsi brings your ancestors back from the grave." The Coca-Cola name in China was first phonetically transliterated as "Ke-kou-ke-la," meaning "bite the wax tadpole" or "female horse stuffed with wax," depending on the dialect. Coke then researched 40,000 characters to find a phonetic equivalent "ko-kou-ko-le", which translates into "happiness in the mouth." And, in Cantonese it's "ho-how ho-lok" – "Delicious and fun."

Gateway to Asia

Gateway Computer's initial foray into Asia was much rockier than expected. The company successfully followed the path from "Dreamer" to "Mm Winner" in the US by making its model of selling computers over the Internet work. Gateway computer has a proven way of individually assembling and shipping PCs to the customer's order. The global BIG M Marketing strategy is fast, efficient, keeps inventory down, and keeps customers happy. In Asia, the company looked at the strengths of its global business model and tailored it carefully to fit the needs of the Asian marketplace, including retail stores to build the brand's profile, and to make sure they had a viable, traditional sales channel until Asian consumers became more comfortable with buying over the Internet. However, Gateway got into the aggressively price-driven PC market relatively late. The retail shops they decided to open for brand exposure were not cost effective to run and did not attract enough customers. The build-and-ship model is easier to execute in the US where UPS delivers everywhere and customers can be reached without going through customs and all 250 million people in the market use the same voltage so no adapters or special ordering instructions are needed. Also, Gateway built a strong brand in the US with their cow-spot boxes. It was too ambitious to build a brand in Asia from scratch, especially in a region where there are so many other US, Taiwanese, Japanese, and other computer makers competing on price-for-performance.

Despite a good effort, the strategy did not catch fire, and Gateway has since moved on to another model, outsourcing all marketing, retail operations and sales to another company.

Examples of theoretically sound strategies that cannot be actually implemented abound, either due to outside factors such as economic slowdowns or powerful competition, or the companies' own inability to execute as planned.

When Fashion Goes out of Fashion

Joyce Ma, the Hong Kong fashion magnate and the founder of the company that bears her name, is from the venerable Asia retailing Ma family that runs the Sincere Department Stores.

Her BIG M Marketing dream was to make international designer fashions available in Hong Kong. For years before Joyce Boutique opened, Hong Kong shoppers (primarily wealthy women but also fashion-conscious men) would travel to Paris, London, Milan, Tokyo, and New York to find the best of European and American fashion. This lifestyle worked well for people with lots of leisure time and disposable income, but was not a practical option for most people looking for international fashions. Although there was some consumer demand for designer fashions to open retail outlets in Hong Kong, the market simply wasn't large enough for most international designers to justify opening their own freestanding stores. For highly established labels such as Christian Dior or Chanel there was sufficient demand, especially when the tourist trade from Japan and Mainland China as well as the Hong Kong local customers were factored in.

For the less well-known, edgier designers, however, the only alternative was to offer a few garments or accessories through department stores such as Hong Kong's Lane Crawford. Being in department stores (even well run, upmarket department stores) presented real problems for the designers. Since the department stores knew that the sales volume of any particular designer's apparel would be low (catering to the tastes of a wealthy niche customer), the designers had to live with the fact that the department store could not justify stocking enough of their range to properly illustrate their full stylistic range and design point of view. For example, a few Helmut Lang or Calvin Klein garments on a rack (available in just a few sizes) or a limited range of Prada handbags in a department store simply does not give the designer a chance to make a statement, and also does not give the customer enough choice.

Into this environment stepped Joyce Ma. Her bold idea had three ingeniously interlocking parts. First, she created a tasteful, modern, upmarket home for fashion, where international designers would feel comfortable selling their designs and seeing them displayed. She built up the designers' trust by launching tasteful marketing campaigns, and expertly displaying the clothing and accessories in store to a high international standard.

Second, she offered her customers the chance to select the latest fashions, hot from the runways of the world, without leaving Hong Kong, and giving them enough choice of designers, styles, and sizes that they could find something that suited them.

Third, although she had to invest in the best shop design, store fit out, furniture, and retail displays to maintain her boutique's image, she had the flexibility to vary her merchandise orders and switch emphasis from one designer to another season to season. By tweaking her portfolio of brands to meet the needs of the customer base she and her team understood so well, she was able to consistently run a profitable business catering both to the clientele that previously would have traveled abroad, and to the more mundane but still discerning (and affluent) customer. Within a short time, Joyce became synonymous with international designer retailing and in the local market what appeared in Joyce (as filtered by Joyce Ma for local tastes from the international shows) became the hallmark of what was "in" for the season.

The designers, who were in absolute control in their home markets and in cities where they had their own stores, in Hong Kong (and later other cities in Asia where Joyce had operations) became simply components of Joyce's successful formula. No one brand was ever indispensable to Joyce's mix, so no single brand ever had an upper hand with Joyce in negotiation or display matters. From a practical business point of view, designer labels were given the opportunity to get incremental sales from a niche group of Asian customers, with the caveat that their overall brand presentation and vision had to be rolled into Joyce's formula.

Joyce stayed in touch with market trends and the changing whims of her customer base. As per capita income in Hong Kong increased, and the demand for international fashions grew stronger in the late 1980s, both Joyce and the international designers saw the opportunity to open freestanding stores for individual designers. For Joyce, this broke with the original concept, but from an operational point of view was an extremely efficient way to run an expanded business. For designers such as Giorgio Armani, the expense of setting up their own operations to run freestanding stores in the region in the late 1970s and early 1980s may not have been immediately justified, but the value of opening freestanding stores to build brand awareness and a loyal customer base was undisputable.

In Joyce, they found a partner who added local value and kept their market access costs relatively low. Joyce knew the local real-estate scene and could select the best locations and negotiate rents and management fees. Joyce knew how to work with contractors and cost-effectively construct world-class stores to the designers' guidelines and expectations. Joyce's buyers traveled regularly to all the top shows, and could buy for the freestanding stores at the same time as they were buying for the Joyce boutiques, saving on staff and travel costs. Joyce was also able to spread and share its shipping/importing expertise and back-office functions such as accounting across several operations. By and large, these were mutually beneficial partnerships and fueled Joyce's drive to become a Hong Kong-listed company, raising capital to expand geographically and increase the number of retail outlets.

In addition to Joyce, there were other companies operating along a similar model to multibrand boutiques, plus operating freestanding stores for individual brands. Christina Ong's Club 21, which originated in Singapore, and the Hong Kong-based Swank Shop both later expanded regionally.

After Joyce's two savvy BIG M Marketing insights (multibrand upmarket fashion boutiques, and operating freestanding stores on behalf of international designers) the company seemed to be pushing forward strongly in little m mode, executing expansion plans and seasonal marketing and promotions plans. The 1997 Asia economic crisis caught many firms such as Joyce in expansion mode at the same time that retail sales were dropping. Two powerful market trends converged to threaten Joyce's long-term viability.

First, as a listed company, shareholders had high expectations that the money raised in the company's flotation on the marketplace would be used to extend the value of the Joyce name and produce good financial returns for the various retail businesses. Shortly after many of the geographic and business expansion plans were complete however, customer demand dropped.

Second, the global brands that had been initially well-served by the Joyce concept started to shift their focus globally (not just in Asia) to freestanding stores and to specially fitted out corners (shops-in-shops) in department stores. Both these trends conspired against the original Joyce multibrand boutique concept. Now that Joyce and others had helped build these international brands and introduced them to a whole generation of fashion consumers, the brands wanted to have more control and also remove a layer in the distribution chain between them and the customer. Having so much of Joyce's value tied up in the relationships with the international designer labels was a double-edged sword as the major labels considered pulling their distribution and retail rights. The international brands also increasingly had options to Joyce as department stores in Asia followed the trend from the rest of the world and offered designer merchandise in branded shops-in-shops.

As the 1997 Asian recession deepened, the international designers realized that although their sales were dropping and the short-term value of their franchises in Asian markets were weakened; the long-term business prospects in the region were good. Many brands took advantage of the temporary slump and the need of their business partners for cash to either terminate their existing retail relationships to buy back the distribution rights to their brands.

Since then, Joyce Boutique has enjoyed continued popularity with the shopping set in Hong Kong, although with ups and downs in the intervening years. At best, Joyce is a textbook case of successful BIG M Marketing, and at worst, a victim of changing market trends and lack of nimbleness in its strategy. In its latest incarnation and after significant turmoil in the late 1990s, Joyce in many ways has lost its special original BIG M Marketing vision, but has settled back into the role of a successful boutique department store.

Coke, Pepsi and Thums Up in India

One of the best examples of BIG M Marketing in action in Asia can be found in the highly competitive Indian soft drinks market. Coca-Cola is not often in the position of finding itself a "Dreamer" company but when the brand returned to the Indian soft drink market after a 16-year hiatus, Coke required a major BIG M strategic marketing push.

For many years, Coke was the leading soft drink in India. Then, in response to the Indian government's requirement that foreign firms own no more than 40% of their Indian subsidiaries (which would have required the company to turn over its secret formula), Coke chose to leave the market in 1977 rather than comply. Pepsi made a similar move, opening the way for domestic Indian brands, such as Double Seven (an early leader) and Campa Cola (by Pure Drinks), which dominated the market in the late 1970s. Thril (by Mcdowells), Double Cola (by Double Cola Manufacturing Company), and Thums Up (from industry leader Parle) joined the fray in the 1980s.

Pepsi returned to the Indian market in 1990 and quickly grabbed 20% of the soft-drinks market and earned market share at the expense of Parle, Pure Drinks, and other domestic companies. The Indian government allowed Pepsi to have 100% equity in its holding company (and the bottling operations they had purchased from local Indian companies) and to market its own products. Pepsi and Thums Up battled it out in what was effectively a two-brand market. Both companies rolled out new packaging and vigorous advertising and promotional campaigns. Then in1993 the Indian government further liberalized the economy to encourage foreign investors, and Coca-Cola re-entered the marketing battle after 16 years by buying the Parle brands (including Thums Up).

Coke immediately captured a large share of the market and Pepsi redirected its attention to combating Coca-Cola (including the Thums Up brand, which in some Indian markets was outselling Coke four to one). However, the main thrust for both companies was to grow the market, and by 1993 annual growth rates had jumped to 20%, compared to 2.5% annual growth in earlier years. There was still ample room for further growth, with per capita annual consumption in India of three bottles compared to 700 bottles in the US.

The two brands squared off in a classic BIG M Marketing strategy confrontation. Pepsi opted to align the brand with Indian events and traditions, sponsoring local sporting events (such as cricket) and festivals, and gave its local managers the authority to make decisions without in-depth input from headquarters. Pepsi also took the lead in cutting prices and offering value-added promotions.

Coke went the national/international route instead, linking itself with major events, including becoming the official sponsor of the 1996 Cricket World Cup, which initially did not prove sustainable or effective. Pepsi cheekily responded with an ad campaign based on the consumer-friendly, accessible tag line referring to their brand: "Nothing official about it."

Coke was also wrestling with brand and bottler issues. Consumers were not waiting for the brand that had left India 16 years before, and Coke was battling with its independent Indian bottlers, many of whom did not wish to sell out to the multinational company. Additionally, Coke focused its attentions (and ad budgets) on Coke rather than its own locally top-selling Thums Up brand, which turned some locals off. Eventually the Thums Up ad budget was increased, but a bungled bungee jumping promotion kept the brand from making further headway. Once again little m Marketing execution proved to be a critical factor.

Since that time, Campa Cola and some of the other former market leaders have been driven off by the Coke/Pepsi rivalry. In India today, the battlefield looks more like the "cola wars" that typifies other global markets, rather than the profusion of local brands. One result of all the BIG M battling has been that both brands are so strong in their marketing that price is the only real differentiator. The combination of increasing package sizes from 250 ml to 300 ml while only raising the price from Rs 6 to Rs 7, or lowering the price on the 250 ml size has hammered 2002 soft drink prices in some Indian markets down to 1997 levels.

When the cola giants were originally allowed back into India, the marketing conflict in the Indian soft-drinks market was driven by BIG M Marketing strategies such as efforts to expand total consumption, setting up effective bottler networks, and understanding the needs of the local consumer. Now, in the more mature market, these companies have moved from being "Dreamers" to "Mm Winners" as their strategies have been matched with relentless little m Marketing such as advertising, event sponsorship, and price cutting.

The moral to be drawn from all of these examples is be a "Dreamer," but make sure you are moving quickly to the right hand side of the quadrant and getting better and better at tactical execution. Having the right strategy is a solid start, but only half the equation. If you are on your way to being an "Mm Winner" then the "Dreamer" quadrant is a good place to pass through. Just continuously monitor both your speed and direction to assure you are not on your way to being a "Doer" or a "Dud."

Mm Winners

"Mm Winners" are companies that serve as examples for the future of marketing in Asia. They match clear customer insight and innovative product development with real world execution. They keep their brands relevant over long periods of time and grow despite fast changing market conditions. They bring together both the vision and the tactical ability to get and keep distribution throughout the region to drive sales. "Mm Winners" in Asia are just as likely to be US or Europe-based multinationals. Sometimes the worldwide experience of a company can give it a tremendous boost in the development of their local strategies. Coca-Cola, Boeing, and Nokia are representative of the power of massive R&D budgets and global best practice. These factors, in conjunction with massive market capitalizations, give them a broad base for success in local markets.

There are lessons to be learned from the companies that are solidly in the "sweet spot" of this quadrant, which have developed both their strategic thinking and their ability to execute to the point to an exceptional degree. Some signs that a company is in the sweet spot include:

- a significant drop in customer complaints;

- increasing profit margins;
- senior management focus on new opportunities rather than sustaining existing operations;
- emphasis on gaining efficiencies and squeezing costs out of your systems;
- competitors are starting to copy your strategy.

Companies here hit a "virtuous spiral" in which the two factors play positively off each other, each accelerating the growth of the other and adding value for the company.

Looking again at some hypothetical companies plotted on the Map, this time in the "Mm Winners" Quadrant 2, Company D, is doing many things right, and is heading into the sweet spot. It has strong strategic marketing and is also executing well against its vision. It is heading up and out on both axes. Dud Company D's management headaches are about delivering consistent performance, finding enough staff that are up to their standards, managing growth, and maintaining a high level of customer service. This company's research and development budget is probably high as a percentage of sales, and is either led by a single visionary leader on whom a dangerous amount of responsibility for the company's success rests, or a large, well-compensated management team. These are all good problems to have, but these issues are as critical to them as to companies that are under performing.

Much more interesting than the companies in the sweet spot, however, are those companies that are on the move.

Company E is frantically executing its plans. The executives must be doing, doing, doing all the time, and the company will very shortly crash through the axis into the "Doers" quadrant if they do not put more focus on strategy. Perhaps Company E has been spoiled by success in a particular category, and is so accustomed to using little m Marketing to reap the short-term benefits of their market position and customer base that they have not taken the time or management attention to refocus their strategy. Or perhaps they are stuck executing an older generation strategy that is working for them now, while in the meantime, their competitors may be innovating with new technology or customer service techniques. This is the type of company called "buggy-whip makers." They may make the best horsewhip, but that makes absolutely no difference if the trend is a shift from horse-drawn carriages to automobiles.

Company F is at a crossroads. Chances are they are not going to be "Mm Winners" for long. The company is going somewhere, and it can be a critical juncture point in the company's history whether they have a soft landing as "Doers" or "Dreamers" or charge full speed ahead into the "Dud" quadrant. Assuming they can't fix everything at once, this company would be well advised to focus on tactical implementation and force themselves into the "Doers" quadrant. The "Dreamers" quadrant is probably not where they want to be. A company rising into the "Dreamer" quadrant has good solid prospects; a company falling into the "Dreamer" quadrant may be spending too much time on trying to reformulate strategy and not enough time on getting the job done.

ILLUSTRATION 3. Mm Winners heading for the Sweet Spot

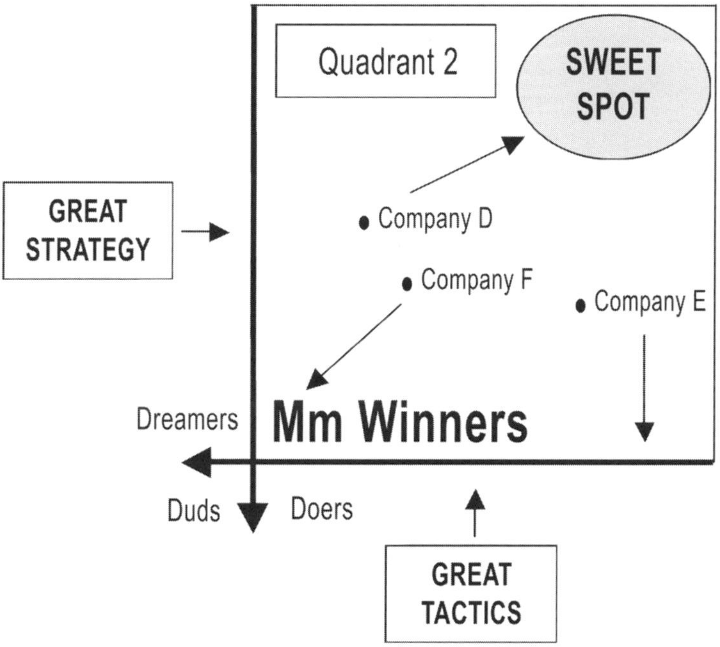

Many savvy Asia companies have market wisdom that allows them to capture BIG M Marketing opportunities that outsiders might not even know exist. This is certainly the case of the traditional *hongs* in Hong Kong, the *chaebol* conglomerates in Korea, and the similar *keiretsu* in Japan. Specific examples are Hutchison Whampoa, Samsung and Sony. These companies have contacts and vertical integration throughout the supply chain that gives them a virtual lock on distribution that is difficult for outsiders to break.

The following section takes a look at the courses steered by some of Asia's "Mm Winners" that have managed to stay relevant and keep growing through rapidly changing market conditions, and have had the executional ability to get and keep distribution throughout the region to drive sales.

Legend in Its Own Lifetime

China's Legend Holdings is solidly in the Mm Winners quadrant. Since 1996, the company has been China's largest PC brand and has built market share on the back of China's rapid PC market expansion, beating out foreign vendors and smaller local companies. Although recent statistics show PC shipments in China increasing at over 60% quarter on quarter, PC penetration is still low relative to the rest of the world. Even as PC growth in China and the region slows, the market is still a fertile marketing area, with more than 5.2 million PCs shipping every year. PC penetration in Asia (excluding Japan) is at 8.9% (2nd quarter 2001 figures), as compared to the US at 51%, so there is further room to grow with increasing need for telecom, computer and network equipment, rising personal incomes, and the dropping of all IT tariffs by 2005. In 2000, Legend also became the leading PC brand in Asia (excluding Japan) with a 9% growth rate and a 12.2% market share.

Aside from being in the right place at the right time, what makes Legend an Mm Winner? The reasons are both BIG M and little m:

BIG M

- The market preference is switching from no name "clone" PCs to branded machines. Legend offers a leading brand name with little/

no price premium over clones, and has a more-than-30% market share compared to the next nearest competitor, Founder, with 9.4%.

- In China, consumers are increasingly buying Legend machines, whereas previously foreign brand name machines had a niche for business use.

- Although many foreign brands team up with local manufacturers, a foreign partner is not necessarily an added competitive advantage in the virtual commodity PC business. The units all run practically the same software and use the same chips. Only four of the top 10 computer brands in China are foreign.

- Legend has matched its PC offering with an ISP (Internet Service Provider) business via China Telecom that allows the company to build its business on the back of increasing Internet access.

- Low-cost production and component bulk purchasing power enable Legend to offer low prices and still make a reasonable margin.

little m

- Legend prices its machines competitively. Especially in the lower-end market where price is a major factor in the purchase decision, low prices will further stimulate demand.

- Legend has China's most extensive PC distribution system. Chances are, wherever you may be looking for a PC, Legend is there, with more than 3,200 agents and distributors.

- Aggressive little m Marketing: across all product lines and markets the company spent 3% of annual revenue on advertising and promotion – the highest in the industry.

- Legend has a marketing and sales program targeted at the 10 million SMEs in China, which are, in the aggregate, major purchasers of PCs.

Legend faces many competitive pressures that threaten to force the company into the "Doers" quadrant, as the industry becomes increasingly price sensitive and commoditized. To remain "Mm Winners," Legend is changing with the demands of the marketplace, and is refocusing the company's vision around being a leading player in Internet access – rather than just PC box manufacturing. Some little m fruits of the company's shifting strategy include linking up with ISPs to drive Web use in China (and to provide a new revenue stream for Legend), and developing new products to meet the new strategy, such as innovative non-PC devices to access the Internet. The company's management is simultaneously relying on these new little m tactics as well as their evolving BIG M Marketing strategy initiatives to keep Legend strong and growing.

Sony: Memory on a Stick

Sony has a proven track record for BIG M, little m Marketing. They have consistently matched high level, global strategies with appealing products and innovative marketing.

The company now has placed a strong worldwide bet that the Memory Stick, the gumstick-sized storage device that can be transferred from PC to printer to digital camera to MP3 player to PDA, will help boost sales of all its product lines and become the defacto standard for this type of convenient, "swappable" storage. This is a proven BIG M strategic gambit: win the battle over the standard and the little m tactics of advertising and promotion become less significant factors in the purchase decision. In the software sector, it has long been realized that common standards are the key to industry success (such as the use of HTML for web pages, and TCP/IP for networking and electronic communication). In the hardware industry, however, proprietary technologies from individual companies are usually left to battle it out to determine the defacto standard.

Sony has engaged in BIG M Marketing standards battles before, both winning (too many times to count) and losing (as with the technically superior Betamax videotape format vs. Matsushita's VHS). And they are not alone. Philips Electronics (in some cases in conjunction with Sony) also has made some brilliantly successful format bids (such as the CD and Compact Cassette) and some less successful ventures, such as the DCC Digital Compact

Cassette format. However, in many ways the losses are the exceptions that prove the rule, because it's clear that the personal and home electronics industry is format-driven, and once the format becomes a standard, product sales follow. For example, and starting with ancient history: 8-track, cassette, Betamax, VHS, DAT, laser disc, video 8, hi-8, VCD, DVD and so on.

With the Memory Stick, Sony is competing against a triple threat: time, alternative technologies, and industry trends. A few years behind the curve, Sony has other competitive flash memory card technologies to deal with, and also an increasing industry trend toward open standards and non-proprietary technology. Although there are potential BIG M Marketing rewards, there is real danger in pursuing a proprietary standard approach. Memory Stick is competing with SmartMedia, Secure Digital, MultiMedia Card, Compact Flash, and others. Sony has also brought out two generations of Memory Stick, which are mutually incompatible. Sony's insistence on standards that are only truly compatible with other Sony devices turns some potential users off. Thinking laterally, Bluetooth and other protocols that allow devices to share information with one another in real time and over "always on" Internet connections are also competitors to the Memory Stick concept, which requires a physical moving of the data holder.

As of this writing, the result of the global standards battle remains to be seen, but with the marketing might, brand power, and distribution clout of Sony behind the initiative, this still has the potential to become another BIG M Marketing success story.

Reinventing Chicken Soup for Generations

BRAND'S Essence of Chicken is one of the few examples of Asia-based brands that have stayed strong and relevant (for more than 165 years!) and today sells more than 100 million bottles annually. This health-food supplement made from whole chickens doubled boiled down to an "essence" is a triumph of BIG M, little m Marketing spanning multiple cultures, decades and company owners. It started as a tonic prepared for England's King George IV, and came to Asia via the British colonies. BRAND'S parent company Cerebos Pacific Limited is listed on the Singapore Stock Exchange, and is 84% owned by Suntory, the Japanese beverage maker. In addition to Cerebos Iodized Table Salt ("See how it runs!"), Cerebos has a portfolio of brand names such as Fountain and Robert Harris, Woh Hup, Horley's, Gregg's, and Asian Gourmet.

People in Asia, however, are most familiar with the company's flagship product - BRAND'S Essence of Chicken, which accounts for over 70% of Cerebos's revenue. Cerebos has a presence across the region, including China, Singapore, Malaysia, Taiwan, Hong Kong, Thailand (Brand's top market, which comprises 35% of total sales), Australia, and New Zealand (although Cerebos is better known for their coffee brands in the latter two markets).

Generations of children – primarily of Chinese extraction – across Asia have grown up with the packets of chicken essence. BRAND'S has evolved into an unusual product that spans a number of diverse and occasionally disparate categories. How can one product be perceived as a treatment for illness, brain food to help children score better on exams, and a gift item all at the same time?

In a bid to keep the product relevant for today's consumers, and perhaps to a more consistent BIG M strategy, BRAND'S has recently been repositioned as a health product ("Partner for Life"), which can be used anytime, by both young and old. In an effort to expand the product's potential to Muslims, the company features the fact that BRAND's is Halal on its packaging in Malaysia and Thailand. The company also touts the fact that BRAND's contains no preservatives or artificial flavoring, and is fat-free, cholesterol-free, and caffeine-free. Research has shown that BRAND'S can increase users' metabolic rate by up to 12% in half an hour. The company's research also highlights the scientific basis for why the product can replenish energy levels, and is good for those who "need extra energy in work, in school or after vigorous sports."

Cerebos has also opted for contemporary sales promotions and sponsorships, such as the 2001 BRAND'S support for the Singapore-Latin America Expedition to Mt. Everest. BRAND'S provided Everest 2001 with a cash sponsorship – and an unlimited supply of BRAND'S for the expedition members. The company also stages outdoor competitions in conjunction with schools to test young people's agility and ability to work together as a team, with cash prizes for the winning individuals and schools.

The healing and brain strengthening properties that some Chinese people attach to chicken essence is a continuing driver of BRAND'S continuing relevance, but clearly that is not enough in itself. This is a company that has managed to keep BIG M and little m Marketing in balance for 165 years.

Hello Kitty – Giving the People what They Want

Certainly one of the quirkiest "Mm Winners" is Hello Kitty. Since 1960, when the Japan gift manufacturer, Sanrio, was founded, the black and white plain line drawing of "Hello Kitty", the cat with no mouth and a red bow, has enjoyed phenomenal licensing success. The company has hit on what seems to be an insatiable consumer for Hello Kitty, her boyfriend Dear Daniel, and her friends Badtz Maru, Monkichi, Pippo Pochacco, and Spottie Dottie. It is hard to make a list of what they have *not* appeared on. An alphabetical selection of the more than 15,000 licensed products includes: bed sheets, cafes, candy, clothing, women's sanitary douches, erasers, eyeglasses, knapsacks, lunchboxes, mobile phone covers, motorcycles, mouse pads, pyjamas, school supplies, stationery, tea sets, toasters, a Tokyo theme park and even a vibrator.

"She's pure license; you can even get a Hello Kitty car! The branding thing is completely out of control, but it started as nothing and maintains its nothingness. It's not about the ego, and in that way it's very Japanese," says Tom Sachs, the artist whose Hello Kitty Nativity Scene created a scandal for some who found the juxtaposition of the religious and the cute to be sacrilegious when it debuted in Barney's department store Christmas windows in New York in 1994.

To keep Hello Kitty fresh, around 600 new products are added every month, and every six months older items are dropped. This keeps consumer interest and broadens the appeal to old and young alike, with a core audience ranging from children to teens. When designs get old, then nostalgia kicks in and they become collector's items for older fans.

Sanrio has brought together an almost addictive BIG M idea with global, sustained little m execution to create a major and highly profitable licensing success.

Being an "Mm Winner" is a precarious position that must be defended everyday. All of these companies have achieved the right balance, but avoiding complacency and sustaining consistency over time, across multiple product lines, and around the region or even the world is an almost impossible job. Every manager who finds their company in the "Mm Winner" quadrant should act every day as if they were "duds" on the way up. To quote Andrew Grove of Intel, "Only the paranoid survive."

Doers

Many companies in Asia can be found in the "Doer" quadrant. "Doers", with their focus on tactics, can earn a lot of money for shareholders and company employees whose bonuses are based on sales volumes. However, the seemingly solid business operations and financial performance of a "Doer" company can mask deeper strategic problems, which need to be addressed for the company to remain viable in the long term. The day-to-day success of "Doers" can blind them to waves of changes coming at them, or lull them into a comfortable state in which they don't have the skills to fend off increasing competition or the flexibility to adapt to new market conditions.

Some "Doers" try to be strategic marketers, while others in this segment put so much focus on sales that they have little concept of what marketing really is. Other "Doers" copy a business model that has proven successful elsewhere and execute it forcefully in their local market. Many of these companies are phenomenally successful through a combination of dogged persistence and door-to-door, shop-by-shop salesmanship. A company can get lucky with its market timing and create a product or service that perfectly captures the needs and wants of the target customer at just that moment. Sometimes the "Doers" succeed because they own the channels of distribution, and can lock out competitors. For every well-connected or lucky "Doer," however, there are dozens of companies that have been born through tremendous effort on the part of their founders, and that have disappeared quietly in a sea of red ink.

The "Doers" include many of the distribution, trading and marketing services companies in Asia. Edward Keller (now part of DiehelmKellerSiber Hegner) has the aim "to access and develop challenging markets". Cycle and Carriage does an effective job of selling and servicing

Mercedes-Benz, Mitsubishi Motors, Proton, and Kia automobiles in Singapore. Companies such as these two are good at what they do in the market niche of creating distribution and building sales channels.

Forceful implementation of little m Marketing has been one of the hallmarks of success in Asia for centuries. Fierce tenacity and resourcefulness are required to get a product to market and push it into the hands of customers. Just getting distribution for a product in a difficult, undeveloped marketplace is no mean feat. This book celebrates the successes of little m Marketing while evangelizing the need to balance this traditional definition of marketing with the overlay of BIG M strategy.

Let's go back to our hypothetical companies, this time in Quadrant 3. "Doer" companies come in many forms. Company G, for example, seems to be doing well. It ranks highly for its tactical skills, and is continuing to move in the right direction on this axis. At the same time, it is rising upwards on the strategy axis. Although there may be no immediate need for management to panic, there is a problem here. The company's outwards and upwards movement signals a misdirection of resources. They are "heading off into space" and simply doing more of whatever they have been doing right in the past, with roughly equal balance between strategy and tactics. Company G needs to re-focus on BIG M strategy to help drive the company upwards at greater velocity into the "Mm Winners" quadrant. On a day-to-day basis there are few signs that Company G isn't doing everything right, but BIG M, little m Marketing Orienteering reveals a more accurate view of the situation.

Company H is in crisis. Perhaps something catastrophic happened to this company or to the market in which it trades. They are heading south on the strategy axis faster than birds in winter, and the company is so close to the tactical axis that there is only a narrow margin for error. Any slight further weakness in their already only average little m capabilities could drive the company into the "Dud" quadrant. Management must take immediate BIG M strategic steps to bolster their marketing, including a rethink of the company's marketing goals and strategies. Companies like H are prime candidates for a takeover, sale, or merger since their main value lies in the company's assets and customers list, rather than their longer-term earning prospects.

Company I is heading for the "Mm Winner" quadrant. The company is clearly doing a lot of BIG M, little m Marketing things right. The only question is why is the company drifting to the left at the same time that it is rising into the "Mm Winner" quadrant? Perhaps management's focus on BIG M strategy has redirected resources from the little m initiatives, and as a result, the tactical aspects of the marketing are losing steam. As long as this trend does not continue and drag the company over in a shallow arch into the "Dud" quadrant, Company I is well positioned for future growth.

The top half of the "Doer" quadrant is a good place to be. The "Mm Winner" quadrant is within reach, and the focus on little m Marketing means that the company is driving sales and working to realize the best returns from its strategy.

ILLUSTRATION 4. Doers

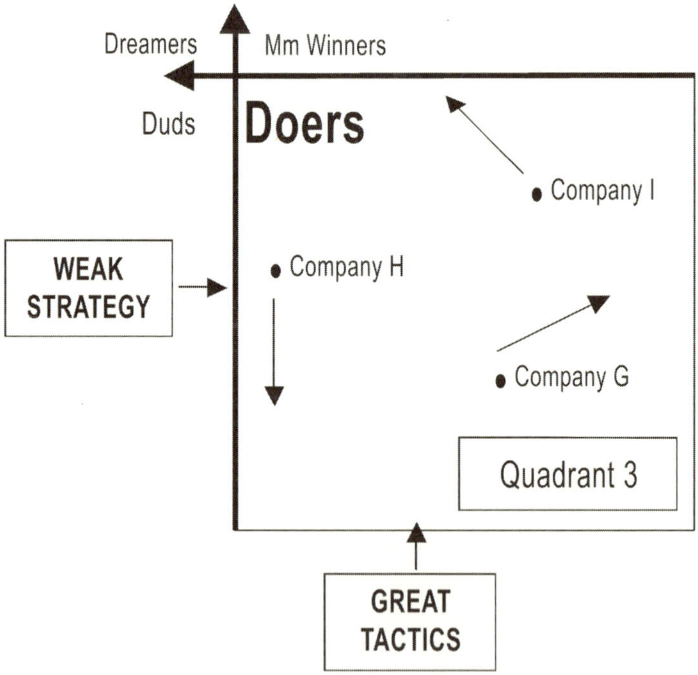

~H_2O+ Hong Kong: Just Add Water

Some of the most effective marketing campaigns are born from a matching of global marketing strategy or brand with local market knowledge and operational expertise. An example of this is ~H_2O+, the water-based skincare brand, which rolled out into Hong Kong and other Asian markets (outside of Japan) with the Hong Kong-based distributor/retailer Water Oasis Company Limited. Although Water Oasis has had its ups (a successful initial public offering) as well as its downs, the company clearly knows how to do retail business in Greater China.

~H_2O+ founder Cindy Melk set out to create a specialty retail environment that would provide a progressive alternative to traditional retail department store shopping. ~H_2O+ is a one-stop skincare shop, offering products for the body from head to toe. The products are designed to appeal to the entire family (women of course, but also men and children) and to the senses – in unique colors, textures and fragrances not found elsewhere.

Water Oasis carefully tailored the ~$H_2$0+ brand's global BIG M Marketing strategy to local market needs. They kept about 85% of what ~H_2O+ had found to be successful in the US, since part of the appeal of ~H_2O+ is that it is an international brand. The "Doers" secret was to know what to do with the other 15%; what to change, and how to change it.

When the right product is introduced in the right way at the right time, with the right promotion, and at the right price, it can look as if bringing a hit brand to Asia is not so difficult. Looking behind the scenes, however, the challenges the "Doer" faces are many and complex, requiring in-depth knowledge of the local market. Water Oasis's success with the ~H_2O+ brand is based on highly-attuned sensitivity to the price and positioning preferences of local consumers, and to skillful retail operations and the ability to identify and negotiate for high traffic retail locations at reasonable prices.

Hong Kong is a challenging environment for marketers. In few places worldwide is there such a dense concentration of sophisticated consumers with such a high disposable income. However, Hong Kong consumers are notoriously fickle and demanding and the ability to understand them and meet their changing needs is critical.

~H_2O+ launched in Hong Kong in May 1998, starting with two stores and then growing to 12, with retail outlets added later in Taiwan and China. Hong Kong was the first market outside the US for ~H_2O+ and grew explosively. Today, the city with a population of 6.8 million still accounts for a larger percentage of ~H_2O+ worldwide sales than all of Japan.

~H_2O+ had some pre-launch "cult" appeal before being launched in Hong Kong, because some leading celebrities had brought ~H_2O+ back with them from overseas and were endorsing the products. This was reinforced by retaining the Hong Kong star Joey Yeung as the local "face" of ~H_2O+. Having local celebrity face in the advertising was a strong draw for local consumers.

Perhaps more important than image was the price positioning. Many Hong Kong people are cost conscious every day about every purchase, and at launch time in 1998 Hong Kong was in the depths of the Asian economic crisis. Water Oasis identified a price gap in the market between the very high-end skincare product lines, and the drugstore brands. The economic downturn became a business development opportunity because although the small elite of top-end shoppers continued to buy status brands (such as European spa products and luxury skincare treatments), many of the younger or less wealthy consumers did not want to or could not afford to spend their money on those brands, so the needs of an entire market segment with disposable income was going unmet.

Water Oasis decided to price ~H_2O+ at a significant premium over drugstore brands, but lower than luxury brands, in order to offer consumers an effective product as well as good perceived value for money for personal use and gift giving. ~H_20+ had a limited marketing budget for the launch, and today still spends a fraction compared with SKII or Shiseido. They decided to do without formal market research since they felt they already knew the market well. The promotional "trigger" for the local Hong Kong market launch was discounting and special offers. At launch time, they offered a HK$200 cash coupon with any purchase over HK$1,000, and conducted special offers with credit-card companies.

Another key factor was the selection of high-traffic shop locations. Water Oasis negotiated hard on rents to assure they had the right cost structure for a profitable business, and then invested in store design and construction.

For the launch and on an on-going basis, Water Oasis has exemplified what a "Doer" company can accomplish with in-depth market knowledge and the ability to roll out a brand's BIG M strategy effectively in the local market. With the right BIG M fundamentals in place, the role of the "Doer" is to execute the little m Marketing in harmony with the local market conditions.

DUDs

"Duds" are companies with no strategic insight and weak execution. In a totally free-market economy, most of these companies would never survive long enough even to earn the label "Dud." However, and particularly in the past, Asia has provided a veritable hothouse for these businesses, which have proliferated under protectionist governments and strong family control. Factors such as cronyism, the use of shell companies to hide assets or earn tax credits, and face-saving exercises on a massive scale, have allowed some businesses to stay alive for decades after they should have imploded under the pressure of market forces. Sectors with more than their share of "Duds" include the Japanese banking industry, Chinese state-owned enterprises, and some family-owned companies in Korea, Indonesia and Malaysia.

Essentially rudderless and profitless, "Duds" by contrast highlight the benefits of responding to the fresh, new marketing atmosphere that is sweeping into the region. Under increasing pressures for free trade and market liberalization, the days of many "Duds" are numbered. Abdullah Badawi, Prime Minister of Malaysia Mahathir Mohamed's appointed successor, acknowledged the issue in a *Far Eastern Economic Review* interview and put it on his agenda for change "I intend to strengthen the current environment of fair play and transparency in the corporate sector. Apart from being morally reprehensible, cronyism distorts efficient allocation of resources and renders politically connected companies uncompetitive and dependent only on government contracts. This flies in the face of enhancing economic competitiveness". For a high profile politician to even address the issue publicly is a sign that the marketing environment is changing.

This book is primarily about celebrating the successes of BIG M, little m Marketing in Asia, and drawing out the lessons companies can use and learn from for their own competitive advantage. Therefore, we will not spend a lot of time on specific "Duds." Instead we'll look at some tell tale warning signs that indicate your company is a "Dud" or that you are doing business with a "Dud."

1. The company's business strategy cannot be articulated and does not make sense unless either the founder or a member of the family that owns/controls the business is present.

2. Credit lines are never a problem, as the company's day-to-day errors are covered by an ever-increasing debt or financing from an unseen source.

3. The local government owns more than 50% of the venture.

4. Inventories are more than 20% higher than the usual average for that industry.

5. Major expansion plans or capital expenditures are approved on the spot without board approval. This may seem like a dream situation – and often is a nightmare.

6. The company's main, stated line of business provides 50% or less of the actual revenue (look out for "consulting and facilitation fees" and extraneous one-time revenue items on the balance sheet).

7. There is not one of your counterparts with whom you are working who you would consider hiring away to join your company.

8. Everyone on the board has the same last name or is related by blood or marriage; Daddy's the chairman.

9. You wouldn't want to buy the company's flagship product or service.

These guidelines are indicators to help you check for danger signs, rather than hard and fast rules. As with any theory, there are many examples of companies that have been successful specifically because they did not follow the conventional wisdom. However, to avoid becoming a "Dud" proceed with caution if your company displays any of the characteristics listed above.

In addition to balancing BIG M and little m Marketing initiatives, companies need to be just plain competent and use common sense, which many do not. For example, a multinational licensing company seized some counterfeit versions of its toys, which had dangerous child-safety flaws. The local executives then contemplated donating to the local orphanage, before wiser heads prevailed. No amount of strategy can save a true "Dud"!

On the BIG M, little Marketing Map, Quadrant 4 is the no man's land of the marketing "Dud." Uninspiring strategy is matched with ineffective tactics. The extreme lower left-hand corner is the "out of business zone." At the extremes of marketing ineptitude, no company can hope to survive. In Asia, some companies in the "out-of-business zone" do struggle on, due to exceptional circumstances, but they are not viable companies. For example, these companies may be:

- propped up by government subsidies;
- have a monopoly position;
- "vanity projects" of family businesses.

Ironically, being a "Dud" is not necessarily a dead end. In fact, "Dud" companies often contain severely undervalued assets and have all the elements required for success, but have not managed to bring them together in any value-producing way. Companies can pass into the "Dud" quadrant for many reasons, such as:

- management neglect;
- loss of direction following a takeover or corporate restructuring;
- resignation of a senior executive;

- changing market conditions that have not been addressed;
- loss of a trade partner or distribution channel.

Plotting the location and movement of three hypothetical companies in Quadrant 4, we can see that Company J is an example of a company that has some traction and momentum that may carry it safely up into the "Doer"category. It is not headed sharply up toward the "Mm Winners" bull's eye, but then that is probably too much to ask from its spot more than half way down the bottom half of the strategy axis. Management has a choice. They can either push very hard on marketing tactical execution to race horizontally into the "Doers" quadrant, or they can split their efforts against improving strategy and tactics. The second option will probably cause the company to move more slowly, but in a higher trajectory that will give it an easier eventual transition to the "Mm Winners" quadrant than if they move quickly into the heart of the "Doers" quadrant. Critical decisions such as this one are usually made under incredible time pressure and are often based on how much financial freedom the company has. The immediate need for sales and gross margin often drives companies to push themselves into the "Doers" quadrant, even though the long-term health of the company would benefit from more focus on BIG M strategy.

If the company can afford to wait another quarter to achieve growth and profits targets, then the emphasis on strategy and tactics simultaneously is probably worth the delay and risk. However, if the company needs to show immediate short-term gains, then a highly tactical "SWAT team" marketing approach is called for.

Company K is toast. Don't waste any more time or shareholders' money. Call in the receivers.

Company L is on a shallow curve up towards the "Dreamer" quadrant. This company, although currently a "Dud," is in pretty good shape. The company's BIG M Marketing strategy probably just needs some refinement to accelerate the upward movement, and it is clear that they are making progress on the tactical front. Company L is still a long way from being an "Mm Winner" but has every chance to get into this quadrant; the shortest and best path is to push into the "Dreamer" category and then slide along into the "Mm Winner" sector. Another route is to push rapidly along horizontally to the left, but that would require remaining categorized as a "Dud" for an extended period of time, which would jeopardize the company's chances for success.

The "Dud" quadrant is the wrong place to stay, but can be an exciting place to be if you have the right BIG M, little m Marketing strategy in place. Being a "Dud" is not necessarily a final sentence. Instead, discovering you are a "Dud" can be a helpful diagnostic and a scary wake-up call that tells you that immediate marketing action is required.

ILLUSTRATION 5. Night of the Living Duds

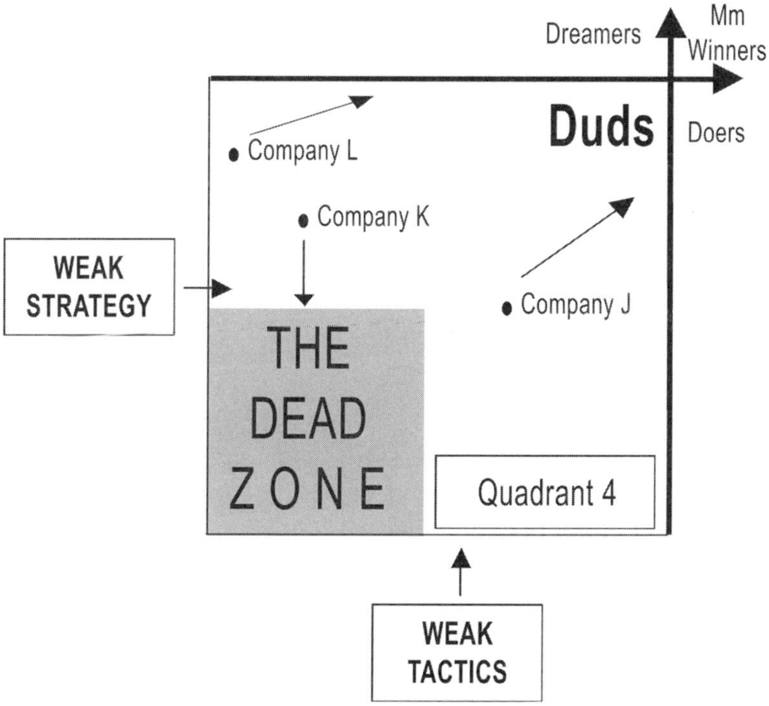

BIG M, little M COMPANIES IN ASIA TODAY

"Only with cutting is jade shaped to use; only with adversity does one achieve the Way."

- Chinese saying

Asia has long served as the manufacturing center for many global brand names, and the logical next step in an Asian company's development is to manufacture the same goods, but under their own brand names, as previously noted. In the early stages of their marketing development, they push commodity products into distribution channels, and focus on little m Marketing tactics that are intended to drive sales rather than actively build a brand. Then in later stages, they work to build true brands with global presence, sales, and reputation.

The China-based color television company Konka is representative of a new wave of Asian companies seeking to become multinationals with recognized brand names. Konka was primarily an export-oriented OEM assembler when it started in the 1980s: 85% of its production was sent overseas under private labels and brands such as GE, Akai and RCA. Only 15% of production was sold domestically in China under the name Konka and three other brand names. In the 1990s, as consumer spending power and demand grew in China, the company changed focus, and eventually became the dominant player in the Chinese domestic colour TV market with Konka-branded goods.

Konka today is working to build up its brand both in China and internationally. At home, Konka faces competition not only from other Chinese television brands such as Chang Hong, but also from international brands that are aggressively seeking to expand their market share in the PRC. This competitive pressure will certainly intensify as the WTO rolls out. At the same time, Konka is making efforts to build a recognized brand internationally, and has moved into the crowded US market, as well as Australia, Russia, India, Indonesia and South Africa. Konka's early positioning in its global rollout efforts has been as a second tier brand (behind Sony and others) and stressing value-for-money as the main brand equity. At this stage in its brand development, Konka's BIG M strategy is clear-cut, and the company is focusing on the little m objective of building international distribution channels and sales and marketing resources in each country.

Konka is one of the latest in an increasing number of worldwide brands with Asia origins that have made the decision to break through to the next level from local brands or OEMs to become brands with Big M saliency and global awareness.

One indicator to assess the progress of Asia companies in developing their global branding and BIG M Marketing savvy is to look at how successful these companies have been worldwide in building their brand awareness and value. The branding consultancy Interbrand conducts an annual survey to measure and track the brand value of the world's leading companies. The survey looks at a company's brand as one of its most valuable assets, on a par with physical plant, cash reserves, patents, and other tangible assets. Interbrand has teamed up with Business Week for the last two surveys, and works with JP Morgan to calculate a financial valuation for brands, and then ranks these brands based on absolute value, the ten highest risers and fallers since the previous study, and other criteria. The 2002 ranking indicates that there are only seven Asia-based companies in the top 81.

Table 2

Rank	Brand	Brand Value 2002 ($ Billiion)	Brand Value 2001 ($ Billion)	% Change	Country
12	Toyota	19.448	18.578	5%	Japan
18	Honda	15.064	14.638	3%	Japan
21	Sony	13.899	15.005	-7%	Japan
32	Nintendo	9.219	9.460	-3%	Japan
34	Samsung	8.310	6.374	30%	S. Korea
43	Canon	6.721	6.580	2%	Japan
81	Panasonic	3.141	3.490	-10%	Japan

Source: Interbrand Corp, J.P. Morgan Chase & Co. 2002.

The highest ranked Asian company is Toyota at number 12. Given Asia's high proportion of worldwide manufacturing (and tremendous dollar value of exports), the fact that no leading Asia-based company ranks in the top 10 brands is an indication that focus on BIG M Marketing still ranks a distant second to little m manufacturing in the region.

Japan is home to six out of the seven Asia-based companies on the Interbrand list Samsung is the only non-Japanese Asian company on the list, at 34th place. Although rising, this ranking is still low considering the large volume and wide range of high quality consumer products the company offers, such as color cellphone handsets and flat-panel TV monitors. The company's BIG M marketing efforts to break out as a powerful global brand known for more than just value-for-money includes spending US$200 million in 2002 on its "DigitAll Experience" marketing campaign, with the decidedly non-exclusive tagline "Everyone's invited". This positioning strategy is being consistently executed across its product lines. Samsung has the potential to climb further in brand value in subsequent surveys.

Of the Asia-based companies on the list, three have decreased in brand value since the last survey, and most remain relatively flat with the exception of Samsung; whose brand rose 30% in value over last year's results, the greatest increase of any of the 100 global brands. None of the Asian brands are new to the list this year.

ImagePower, a revealing survey conducted in 2000 by Landor Associates, the international corporate identity and branding consultancy, evaluated 250 technology brands in the US and 125 technology-related brands in markets around the world. The survey tests consumers around the world for their impressions of brands based on the following attributes:

- Share of mind: How familiar are consumers with the brand?
- Share of heart: Which brands speak to their target consumers like no others?
- Distinctiveness: Which brands turn consumers' heads?
- Appropriateness: How well does a brand fit the target audiences' needs?
- Momentum: How successful will the brand be in the next few years?

By these criteria, Sony has reached the status of a global brand that happens to have an Asia headquarters, rather than being an Asia brand. Sony shared the top spot on the list, along with Microsoft.

These rankings suggest that there is ample scope for Asia-based companies to increase their use of BIG M Marketing. Many of these companies have grown internationally primarily as OEMs and exporters, and their track record for marketing-based success still lags behind the global standard. The trend is moving in the right direction, and companies such as Sony have shown that they can make the transition from product and price-based businesses to BIG M, little m Marketing-driven brands. Samsung is working to build a similar franchise, and as we saw at the beginning of this section, brands like Konka are just at the early stages of this process.

New Zealand's Zespri International's experience with kiwi fruit is an example of an entire industry working to build a global brand to rise above the brutal price-based competition among commodity products. The New Zealand Kiwi Marketing Board created the Zespri name in 1996 to brand the nation's kiwi fruit and help drive exports. The kiwi was originally known as the Chinese gooseberry (*yang tao).* Brought to New Zealand in the 1800s, it was renamed kiwi fruit in the late 1950s. However the name kiwi was never trademarked, so the switch to Zespri was in part an effort to create an ownable equity for the New Zealand growers. Now there is even a Zespri Gold, as the fruit marketers borrow a few branding lessons from their colleagues in the Fast Moving Consumer Goods (FMCG) sector. Zespri International, the grower-owned kiwi fruit producer, sells two billion kiwis worldwide annually, and this branding exercise and aggressive little m Marketing support helped New Zealand compete against other kiwi growers and exporters in Australia, California, Chile, and Turkey.

Asia's *Media* magazine conducted the 2002 Asian Brands Poll, asking its readers from the marketing, advertising and promotion industries to help assess the state of brand development in Asia. Readers identified the following Asian brands as the ten most familiar:

- Cathay Pacific
- Shangri-La

- HSBC
- Singapore Airlines
- San Miguel
- Mandarin Oriental
- Wellcome
- Peninsula
- Park'n Shop
- Watson's Water

In the same survey, readers identified HSBC, Singapore Airlines, Cathay Pacific, China Mobile, and Park'n Shop as the most successful brands.

The *Media* rankings show strength and movement among Asia-based brands, however the real test of BIG M, little m Marketing progress will be when these brands start appearing more frequently and higher in the global valuation rankings. The potential of brands to expand outside of their home and regional markets was succinctly summed up in a cultural context by French philosopher Alexander Kojeve in 1959. When describing Japan, he said "The interaction of the West and Japan will result not in a vulgarization of Japan but rather in a Japanization of the West."

At the beginning of this section, we looked inside the rising Chinese brand Konka. As with the rising Japanese brands of previous decades, and Korea's Samsung more recently, China may well be the source of some of tomorrow's global BIG M, little m Marketing successes. Much of the dynamic of BIG M, little m Marketing relies on the forces of a free market economy. Despite pockets of state-sanctioned "capitalism with Chinese characteristics" in Guangzhou Province, Shanghai and elsewhere, by and large, China still has a limited market economy. The ongoing rule of the Communist Party and effects of deeply ingrained socialist theory mean that the individual manager is rarely in a position to impact BIG M decision-making. The strategic marketing decisions are not made at the level of the individual worker, manager, or even the individual company; they are matters of policy determined at the city, provincial or national government level. Although in certain sectors entrepreneurialism is flourishing, the little m mindset is continually reinforced by state-owned firms' restraint on managerial decision-making.

Marketing in China is still largely the process of controlling and directing distribution, so that required products are available to businesses and consumers in the right place at the right time. Although some Chinese products are well branded, often the promise the brand makes is not the main reason for its commercial success. Widespread distribution or support from a state-owned enterprise is likely to be the primary cause. However, there is some evidence that the Chinese market is on the road from product orientation to brand development.

According to a 2001 survey, Hongtashan cigarettes is the most valuable Chinese brand (for the seventh year in a row), rated at 46 billion yuan (US$ 5.6 billion). Other top valued brands were Haier (household appliances) at 43.6 billion yuan (US$5.3 billion), Changhong, Wuliangye liquor, and TCL. The annual average sales for the most valuable brand in the survey rose 39.7 % over the previous year, and brand value increased by 15.1% on average.

With these valuations as a starting point, how long will it take for these Chinese brands to begin to rival the world's super brands? Some obstacles are posed by competition from international brands making inroads in China post WTO, according to the *People's Daily* newspaper. For international consumer brands in China, demand and brand reputation can drive sales, sometimes fuelled by the influx of "gray market," smuggled or parallel import goods. For example, genuine Kodak film is available throughout China, although often it is brought into the market by businesses that have no connection whatsoever with the parent company. Domestic competitor Lucky Film, a state-owned enterprise, has a 20% share of the domestic market, but still lags behind imported Fuji and Kodak. To stay competitive and continue building market share, Lucky Film Group believes that Chinese companies must focus on their best products, and overlay the strengths of their Chinese management with some overseas marketing methods. Of course with Chinese film consumption at 0.10 rolls of film per person per year, compared with four rolls per person in developed countries, the opportunity lies more in expanding the entire photographic market than grabbing market share from competitors.

Another example of gray market distribution is Marlboro cigarettes, which are imported under a strict quota imposed by the China government, though the market penetration of the brand is much greater than that quota. Illegal importers fulfill the additional demand with authentic product smuggled into China from other markets.

Whatever the challenges from international brands, given the 20-30% annual growth rates (comparing the sales of the top 2001 brands against their 2000 performance), Chinese brands will be challenging Global Top 500 brands in terms of brand value in around four years time. In the new marketing environment, will we have to wait very long before Hongtashan becomes the next Marlboro, or Haier the next Sony?

Trends and the Future

"Sitting in front of his master, the student posed the question, 'All the mountains, rivers, lakes, the earth, the sun, the moon, and the stars, where do they come from?' In answer, the master replied, 'Where does your question come from?'"

- Zen story

The many powerful forces for change that are gathering momentum in the region provide opportunities for the aggressive BIG M, little m Marketer, and will certainly accelerate the pace of more open competition, as they make up markets more susceptible to the impact of marketing strategy. BIG M strategy will play an ever-increasing role and will become increasingly integrated with the tactics. The sophistication of marketing will not advance at the same rate across all countries, and some of the most significant trends are global rather than originating in Asia. The forces at work are both macro and micro-economic, and political and social. Some of the most important are:

- growth of outsourcing
- supply chain management
- human resources
- impact of the WTO – especially in China and Taiwan
- increasing economic freedom
- spread of Internet access

This section provides a brief overview of these trends and their implications for marketing.

Outsourcing

Outsourcing has long been an important part of the growth of Asian economies due to all the manufacturing that is subcontracted from the West to Asia-based companies. Outsourcing has two distinct dimensions: manufacturing and business process outsourcing (the long-term contracting of non-core business functions to specialized service providers). Japan, Korea, Singapore, Taiwan, and China have all built local industries based on contract manufacturing for international brand names. The size of the outsourcing market in Asia is roughly the same as in the US and in Europe, and is growing at about the same rate. The difference in Asia is that the bulk of the outsourcing marketplace is still comprised of manufacturing; but the future growth potential is in business-process outsourcing.

Manufacturing outsourcing was once a major contributor to Asia's emphasis on little m Marketing in that Asia-based companies simply produced products for multinational vendors, without developing brands of their own. Since then, Japan has built a portfolio of world-class brands such as Sony, Toyota, and Ajinomoto through intensive research and development, and marketing execution. Korea has begun to make the switch from contract manufacturing to creating global brands such as Hyundai and Samsung. Although Hong Kong has been home to local manufacturing, its strength has always been as a trading center for goods originating in China. As a result Hong Kong has produced no world-class brands, and the few brands that have been developed in Hong Kong only have local relevance, such as the mass market Café de Coral fast-food chain.

Singapore has followed a similar path, although some firms there have created regionally or globally relevant brands such as Tiger Beer, Singapore Airlines, BRAND'S Essence of Chicken, and Tiger Balm, which serve as the exceptions to the rule.

The increasing use of business process outsourcing (such as professional services) is illustrated by such successes as the Indian IT industry. India's software industry is now one of the most competitive in the world. It has grown explosively in two directions. First, customers from around the world have come to rely on Indian software solutions that combine world-class programming and technical skills with good value. Second, demand has also grown in the country's own domestic market. The sector has grown with technical, marketing, and infrastructure assistance from the government, but without any protectionist measures since 1984. The industry's growth depends on the country's ability to draw on the world's second largest pool of scientific manpower (after the US). Another example is the publishing industry in the Philippines. Some publishing ventures have located their editorial teams in the Philippines to give them low cost access to excellent writers.

Professional service outsourcing is relatively new on the business scene, and allows businesses in Asia (either Asia-based or multinationals) to tap into best-practice skills and expertise, and the marketing field is no exception. Using marketing consultants, research firms, sales promotions specialists, and ad agencies, outsourcing can reduce costs as compared to developing the same expertise in-house, but perhaps more importantly, allows companies to focus on their core business while simultaneously enhancing market reaction time and providing access to specialist branding/marketing/product development skills and innovation.

Singapore-based Batey Ads is one pioneer in this area in Asia with the creation of the long-running Singapore Airlines "Singapore Girl" ad campaign, while the influx of international advertising and public relations agencies further accelerated the trend. Today, specialist consultancies such as the brand identity consultant Landor Associates (which created the Cathay Pacific "wing" identity) are available to just about any Asian enterprise that has the trust in outsourcing, and the budget, to hire them.

Additionally, the outsourcing of non-core but essential, specialist functions, ranging from day-to-day back office administration (such as payroll processing) and supply chain management to human resources and customer relationship management, frees up companies to focus on the demands of their marketplaces, their customers needs, and on building brands. Both Asia-based companies and multinationals operating in the region can outsource many functions so they can operate regionally and build their businesses without having to build a local infrastructure in every country.

The research firm IDC expects that Asia's business process outsourcing market (including application and process outsourcing and integration services) will more than double from US$3.2 billion in 1999 to US$6.9 billion in 2004. The opportunity for Asian businesses is to view outsourcing services to third party experts as a strategic tool to enhance their competitiveness, rather than as an indication of their own internal weakness. Multinational outsourcing consultancies such as EDS and the management of US and Europe-based multinationals who already see the benefits of outsourcing are important evangelists in the process of bringing the benefits of the practice into the region.

Supply Chain Management

As distribution systems become more efficient, funds are freed up to invest in marketing, rather than simply paying the bloated costs of getting a product into the marketplace. In virtually every industry from the Chinese insurance industry to the Malaysian liquor industry, supply chain management is going to be a powerful force for BIG M Marketing innovation.

When product distribution systems depend on personal relationships and organic growth, there are bound to be inefficiencies. In many Asian economies, the path a product takes from factory to retail shop floor is Byzantine, with numerous unnecessary layers in the distribution process and middleman companies that add cost but little value as they handle the product. When markets are not free and marketing is primarily driven by tactics, no one has a clear view of the entire supply chain and no one looks at the total picture to plan for cost effectiveness.

The increasing penetration of supply chain management in Asia is driving inefficiencies out of the system, lowering costs, raising profit margins, and providing a more level playing field where good marketing can make the difference between a product's success or failure. For example, the Korean grocery market used to comprise a long chain of wholesalers, distributors, sub-distributors and "mom-and-pop" stores, reaching from the farm or food-processing plant down to the local neighborhood. None of the local retail stores ever had enough buying power individually to bargain for reduced prices. Every link in the distribution chain represented income for individual distributors and re-sellers, income that they were naturally reluctant to give up for the sake of the efficiency of the overall distribution system. The Korean grocery market is still in the process of shaking out, as mass market outlets with massive buying power and direct access to manufacturers and wholesalers are putting increased pricing pressure on the entire system.

Throughout the region, supply chain management is becoming an increasingly important management discipline, and a raft of consulting businesses and software companies (such as Manugistics and i2) are rushing to educate the market and meet demand.

Human Resources

The years ahead of increasing competition and transparency will truly stretch the region's ability to manage and develop human resources in Asia. BIG M, little m Marketing success is directly linked to the quality of strategic thinking and executional expertise of the management and marketing teams. Some crucial factors to assure a supply of BIG M, little m Marketers include the need for educational institutions to offer the right curriculum, the availability of workers with local and international education and experience, the balance of local and expatriate staff, and the privatization of many formerly nationalized industries so that the profit motive becomes foremost in companies' decision making processes.

With the greater transparency and openness in Asian business, some of the previous generation of executives may not have the relevant perspectives and skills sets to meet the BIG M, little m Marketing challenge. Some younger executives and those trained or educated abroad have been exposed to the demands of the new competitive environment, and may have had exposure to world-class marketing case studies and practices. The pressure to upgrade the level of Asian marketing executives does not just come from the internal countries' marketplaces. The region has become one of the United States' most strategic trading areas. For example, two of the US's leading exporters, Microsoft and Boeing, will soon do more business in Asia than in the US, and will require ever increasing numbers of BIG M, little m Marketers to fulfill their companies' marketing potential in the region.

These companies and other multinationals have changed their style from firefighting (responding to urgent needs for scarce staff) to planned and organized executive recruiting. When multinational companies initially recognized the opportunities in China, they moved quickly to hire people with excellent English skills, who were often expatriates or returning Chinese emigrants. Today, English proficiency is not as relevant, and recruitment is based on competence, with more focus on creativity and the willingness of candidates to put in extra effort.

This trend is perhaps most visible now in China. Executives with world-class professional skills (whether expatriate or local) will be in increasingly higher demand, and will put pressure on schools and universities to deliver highly qualified graduates. People in more labor-intensive industries will likely drop further to the wrong side of the divide. This rising demand could bring on a new era of expatriate hiring as the available pool of talented, qualified local hires is dried up by the rapid rate at which central business functions are being localized (particularly in infrastructure development industries such as telecommunications).

As the demand for local hires continues to increase, the gap between the total compensation received by local hires and expatriates is narrowing, and is in many cases nonexistent. Although recruiting executives into companies is a major task, the real challenge –and measure of success – is whether they stay. High staff turnover is expensive for any company, and meeting the employee's expectations about their career opportunities and the working environment are increasingly important ways to encourage retention and reduce human resources cost. For example, multinationals in China have moved quickly to help their local executive teams adopt global best practices in general management, human resources and sales. However, staff retention in the operations and finance areas has proven more difficult.

Since the definition and use of marketing varies among different cultures, the localization of the marketing function is simultaneously the most important and the most difficult. Cost considerations should not be the force that brings on localization. Instead, localization should be a continuous and natural evolution that multinationals undertake when they have the right critical mass of business and rising needs for executives with well rounded skills and experience, such as BIG M, little m Marketing.

The previous distinctions between "local = cheap, and expatriate = expensive" are now outmoded. Rarely are expatriates now offered hardship allowances for China while the top 5% of local executives will command a compensation premium for their services. Although salaries for comparable positions still lag behind compensation benchmarks from the West, star performers from successful local companies now represent value for money, rather than being cheap to hire.

China, Taiwan and WTO

As noted previously, one of the biggest changes to Asia's marketing landscape is China and Taiwan's accession into the WTO. With the WTO comes an increasingly competitive trading environment that offers significant BIG M

Marketing opportunities for Chinese and Taiwanese companies to achieve competitive advantage, and for multinational companies to increase their exports. The progressive lowering and removal of cross national tariff and non-tariff barriers means that strategic marketing has increasing importance as the value of contacts and relationships as guaranteed business drivers simultaneously diminishes. As the trading environment becomes continuously more transparent, effective execution is still necessary for success, but the more level playing field provides opportunities for new, qualified entrants to gain market share. In addition to opportunity, the WTO also brings pain as previously protected industries, market positions and jobs are swept away or re-aligned under the pressure of increased competition.

China

The provisions of the WTO give China tremendous scope for gaining a larger share of low cost manufacturing as import quotas are dropped. At the same time, marketers at Chinese companies will increasingly need to rise and meet the challenge of competing with multinational brands, which will certainly sharpen both BIG M and little m Marketing skills. Multinationals importing goods into China for the first time will have direct access to the marketplace in many sectors. Simultaneously, domestic companies such as Legend computer are now taking advantage of their increased access to overseas markets. The next 10 years will be marked by tremendous change as today's leaders and tomorrow's challengers jockey for competitive advantage both in China and abroad.

China is expected to continuously accelerate the pace of import growth. For example, between 1990 and 2001, US annual exports to China more than tripled, especially in such infrastructure and B2B sectors as electrical machinery, fertilizer, and medical and power generation equipment. The trend continues, with the US trade deficit with China decreasing to US$8.5 billion in June 2002. Although still a sizable deficit, this statistic needs to be viewed against a background of increased exports, and also includes the Entrepot trade (goods shipped from one economy to another through a third economy for further processing or assembly) through Hong Kong, which causes the US bilateral trade deficit with China to be overstated by 20% or more.

Multinationals in China

In China, the demand for businesses that can deliver goods and services to international standards is already there, and multinationals are now beginning to find ways to go directly to their customers, bypassing the traditional local middlemen when and where that layer represents inefficiency or adds additional expense to the distribution chain. Multinational companies in many industry segments can now go directly into the market with their own more familiar and perhaps more efficient distribution and financial systems. At the same time, Chinese industries now require access to these same services and a broad range of business support services such as accounting and management consulting, as they race to upgrade the quality level of their local marketing and export operations to more rigorous international standards.

The automotive industry in China is an example of an industry already undergoing significant change. The protectionist measures and domestic regulations that originally kept distribution costs high also kept car prices high. Pent-up consumer demand from the pre-WTO era for lower-priced vehicles is starting to accelerate sales. Ford Motor Company anticipates in a very short time a six-fold increase in the ratio of truck to car sales (currently 70% trucks and 30% passenger cars), shifting towards the 50-50 mix seen in other world markets. Under the WTO ground rules, starting in 2002 up to US$6 billion worth of vehicles and components each year can be imported into China, 10 times the pre-WTO level, and this will increase by 15% every year until phase-in is complete. Few markets in history have experienced such a dramatic and immediate shift in the marketing environment.

Chinese Companies at Home and Abroad

WTO membership will also push Chinese companies at home to focus more on the customer. There will be more competitive pressure from overseas brands, but also more financing support available to upgrade business infrastructure and service. The new competitive situation will not force overnight change in China, but will create a strong incentive to Chinese businesses to upgrade both the level and strategic value of marketing in their organizations.

Reciprocally, as foreign companies gain greater access to the China market, Chinese companies will also have greater access to export markets. For example, the gradual dropping of textile quotas will allow China the opportunity to take back manufacturing market share from other countries, which have built industries locally to make use of their quotas and scoop up business China has been previously blocked from taking. This renewed competitiveness will spark the need for BIG M international Marketing by both the Chinese companies and their overseas competitors.

Beyond China

The WTO has already started transforming the marketing landscape in Asia among member countries and the overseas companies that export to them. China's accession to the WTO is not only a boost to the Chinese economy, but also to other countries in Asia which have renewed opportunities to build their businesses behind China's lowered trade barriers. Taiwan joined the WTO immediately after China, which raises potential BIG M Marketing clashes as well as synergies across the straits of Fujian. In Taiwan, SMEs comprise more than 98% of the island's one million registered enterprises, employ just under 80% of the island's total work force and can be credited for creating half of Taiwan's aggregate export value. The WTO opens up even more opportunities for those Taiwanese SMEs that can fast and flexibly change their BIG M and little m Marketing to rush into gaps in the marketplace that offer business potential, without now having to worry about quotas.

The BIG M possibilities for competitive advantage will open new opportunities across many industries. Automotive and consumer products have already been mentioned. Here are some others:

Financial Services

American banks can make local currency loans to Chinese enterprises two years after China's WTO entry, and enter the retail banking market after five years. Foreign carmakers will be allowed to offer vehicle financing, and insurance companies will also benefit. This competitive pressure in the marketplace will drive some companies out of business, and drive up the value of others as the markets open up.

Manufacturing, Tech, and Retail

Companies involved with telecommunications (including the Internet), the semiconductor industry, chemical companies, major manufacturers (such as Boeing) and global retailers are expected to benefit from new opportunities for growth.

Professional Services

Demand for lawyers, business consultants, accountants, and architects is expected to rise among multinationals as these sectors increase their need for support services. At the same time, companies in Chinese counterparts will require similar services to help drive their exports.

Although China is the center of much of the WTO attention, the competitive pressures that will come with the new trading order will be felt throughout all countries and vertical markets. As markets become freer, BIG M, little m Marketing will increasingly provide points of differentiation and competitive advantage.

Economic Freedom

The fact that many Asian economies are becoming increasingly free as governments diminish their market control is a powerful driver of BIG M, little m Marketing. The trend, however, is inconsistent across the region with some economies advancing and others slipping into further control.

One measure is the annual "Index of Economic Freedom" survey from The Heritage Foundation and *The Wall Street Journal.* The survey ranks economic freedom on a range of economic indicators including government spending as a proportion of GDP, the rule of law, and government intervention and monetary policy. In the 2002 survey, Hong Kong held onto its title as the world's freest economy. Four of the world's top 10 freest economies are in Asia Pacific. Six Asian countries (North Korea at 155th and overall last place; Vietnam, Burma, Turkmenistan, Uzbekistan and Laos) also made the list of 10 *least* free economies in the world.

The rankings for Hong Kong (#1) and Singapore (#2) match with the findings of other studies, such as the US-based Cato Institute and Canada's Fraser Institute's "Economic Freedom of the World 2002" survey, which was originally started with the help of Nobel Laureate Milton Friedman.

Despite its high rankings, Hong Kong is home to a BIG M, little m Marketing contradiction. In many ways the bustling economy is a breeding ground for entrepreneurialism and marketing innovation. Its status as one of the trade gateways to China (with Shanghai and others nipping at its heels) makes it special, even if not as unusual a landmark on the world economy as in the days when it was a British colony. It has a free-spending consumer base and a solid per capita GDP comparable to wealthy European countries.

On the other hand, it is a small market (population 6.72 million in mid 2001) and some individual sectors don't seem competitive at all, especially in the consumer sector. For example, there are just two significant supermarket chains in Hong Kong, and attempts by others to enter have failed. Hong Kong *still* has tremendous potential for business-to-business BIG M, little m Marketing, although the major boost the WTO gives to China, Taiwan and the rest of the region may contribute to the diminishment of Hong Kong's role as a regional gateway.

According to the "Index of Economic Freedom" survey, in the last year overall economic freedom in Asia declined. Ten countries were rated as freer and 17 as more repressed than the previous year. However, Hong Kong and Singapore held onto their top two ranked spots, and Thailand rose from 46th to 27th place.

Asia has some of the most dynamic markets in the world, and the little m Marketing tactics that helped carry these economies through their formative years will have to be augmented by BIG M strategies going forward to take maximum compctitive advantage from the even greater economic freedom the WTO era dictates.

The Internet

Despite the highly publicized bursting of the dotcom bubble, the Internet is still one of the most powerful forces driving BIG M, little m Marketing opportunities. For centuries in Asia business power was equated with wealth, contacts, exclusivity and access to carefully guarded channels of communication and distribution. The Internet is starting to bash down barriers to commerce and putting the tools of buying and selling in the hands of the masses. There has been confusion in the marketplace between the short-term collapse of technology-based stock prices and the longer-term potential of the Internet to help drive business strategy. As over-hyped tech stock values collapsed, new Internet-based business models have taken longer to create change than the "overnight successes" their founders envisioned. However, technology and the Internet are here to stay as powerful and transforming forces. A good analogy is the post office. Mail has been essential for most businesses for hundreds of years but no one ever asks if you have a postal strategy. It's just there and you use it. That's the way it is with the Internet.

Even pure play businesses on the Internet face competitive pressures from new challengers. Commercial Websites can change their content, graphic design, and functionality on an hourly basis with relatively little incremental expense. They can spot trends and shift to meet customer demand on a continuous basis. The competitive problem is that every company in the industry can do the same thing and the barriers to entry are relatively low. Portals are also facing competition for "eyeballs" from search engines that are many people's first port of call on the Web and from private individuals who put together weblogs (or "blogs") – carefully compiled lists of interesting sites and links to information on the Web. People post their links simply because they want to share, not to make money via advertising or subscription charges.

Now everyone has access to becoming a publisher and a businessperson, as well as a consumer. An e-commerce business can be started with a Hotmail account, and buyers and sellers are brought together in an efficient, virtually frictionless way. A small businessperson can run an entire business through an auction website such as eBay, or Eachnet.com in China. Traditional businesses are faced with both threats and opportunities. For example, the *South China Morning Post* has among the strongest classified advertising businesses in the world and for years provided a marketplace for goods and services. Now that many of the functions of classified advertising are being taken over by Web-based marketplaces and online services, the publisher is responding by making respected new economy inroads with the website SCMP.com.

Quicker than a Grande Latte

Starbucks is one traditional retailer that is harnessing the BIG M potential of the Internet. In Singapore, Starbucks wanted to identify a group of customers for e-mail marketing campaigns. They asked the portal Microsoft MSN to design an open-ended data capture campaign, which centred on a survey of users. The campaign used a series of simple but provocative text links on MSN Singapore's Entertainment channel. When users clicked on the text link they were asked to provide personal information and e-mail address and to complete a survey. After completing the survey, they received a thank you message and a printable coupon for a free drink at Starbucks.

Within two days of the campaign's inception, more than 12,000 people had participated in the online survey, and with the allotted coupons already exhausted, Starbucks decided to end the campaign early. MSN received 72% of the total responses across all three sites that ran the survey. In a matter of days, Starbucks collected a detailed personal profile of customers and their coffee-drinking habits.

Power in the People's Mouse

Perhaps even more important than the communications power the Internet puts in the hands of corporations is the power Internet puts in the hands of just about everyone. Traditionally in Asia, gaining control of media has been part of just about every business conglomerate's and government's plans. For example, Samsung in Korea owns the *JoongAng Ilbo* newspaper. In Hong Kong, the Kuok family controls the *South China Morning Post*. In Singapore the government owns Singapore Press Holdings and its various subsidiaries. Just because powerful forces own these media does not necessarily mean they lack journalistic integrity, but the ownership of mass media can provide a channel for the editorial point of view of the owners.

Putting aside any political or propaganda implications, the impact on marketing in the region has been subtle but pervasive. The owners and publishers of traditional media are in absolute control of the information that is "broadcast" out to viewers and readers. The Internet gives every individual businessperson, SME and corporation the same access to information, and also turns every individual into a publisher. For US$2,000, a clever marketer can create a website that is as functional and appealing as one that costs 10 times as much. Japanese teens trading SMS messages on their mobile phones are as likely to shape the image and success of a brand as television advertising. The viral nature of Internet marketing is accessible to all, and big business's access to established resources or contacts does not mean necessarily that big business will be better at the task than small business.

The Internet is a good match with the entrepreneurial energy of most Asian cultures, and puts an awesome box of both BIG M and little m Marketing tools in every businessperson's hands. The potential of a Taiwanese "Digital Nightmarket" or a Korean "Digital Namdaemun" (one of Seoul's two large marketplaces) as well the staggering amount of strategically useful marketing information freely available on the Web is incalculable. A visit to the Hong Kong Trade Development Council's website at www.tdctrade.com provides more free, instantly accessible and well organized information than a corporation's in-house department could assemble in a year of work. Search engines yield massive amounts of sifted data with minimal effort. A recent search for "Sri Lanka shipping agents," for example, on Google (www.google.com) in .29 seconds provided 5,610 responses and led directly to the category "Business > Industries > Transportation > Maritime > Services > Agents, Brokers and Charterers." The user is also given the choice of selecting "Bunkers and Bunkering" or "Buying and Selling Ships." This is an astonishing amount of detailed information to be available to everyone. For the shipping entrepreneur to be successful in Sri Lanka, the deciding factor will no longer be access to information, and a multitude of BIG M Marketing opportunities is opened up.

From Bricks to Clicks

Established businesses in Asia have also discovered the Web. For example, SESAMi Inc (www.sesami.com), owned by SingTel and a portfolio of Hong Kong's leading trading companies, provides online B2B marketplaces that not only use the power of the Internet to automate and match up traditional business transactions, but also offer (for a revenue-generating fee) access to that marketplace to other companies. Li & Fung is another example of a company that has moved quickly and effectively to build a strong online B2B presence. Growing from an old-line sourcing business, Li & Fung now manages supply chains for high-volume, time-sensitive consumer goods, including garments, sporting goods, and toys. Their customers include many of the world's leading brands, and sourcing takes place across 37 countries.

Geographic Powerhouses

Powerful forces are emerging to drive the growth of dynamic, regional businesses. At the same time that the WTO and increased cross border trade are working to break down international barriers, the new environment of heightened competition is also likely to force a rise in nationalism. In just about every country in Asia, local businesses will simultaneously have more competitive pressures in their domestic markets from international businesses and increasing business opportunities overseas. Most countries in Asia have had national trade promotion efforts in place for some time (such as Taiwan's "Innovalue" campaign) to drive foreign investment and exports. Increasingly, both trade-marketing efforts for countries and individual businesses in the region will have to expand the scope and intensity of their initiatives to keep and build their market share. In this process, the smartest BIG M, best-capitalized marketers will grow into true regional (and perhaps global) businesses, while the same forces will drive others out of business. This competition will be healthy, and drive the increasing sophistication of Big M, little m Marketing .

Japan – Now and for the Foreseeable Future

In many ways, "Japan Inc." blazed the trail for other Asian national and corporate marketing efforts to follow. Looking at *Fortune* magazine's Asia's Top 50 list (as part of their Global 500 list), the first 13 of the top companies (in 2001 revenues) are all Japanese. State Power of China is the first non-Japanese company on the list at 14. Overall, 39 of the 50 are Japanese. And, as we saw with the world's most valuable brands survey, six of the seven Asian companies that made the top 100 are Japanese. Setting aside structural, macro-economic factors such as land scarcity and high real estate prices in Japan, which drive up the total turnover of Japanese enterprises to levels artificially higher than what one would find in lower cost economies, there is no doubt that Japan's model is successful and a template for other Asian economies and companies.

Here's an outline of the transition many Japanese manufacturers have undergone over the years. After World War Two, Japanese domestic companies fueled their growth by serving as contract manufacturers for multinationals. Over time, they added value at increasingly higher levels in the value chain (moving from assembly to design and later innovation). These companies then began saturating their own home markets with locally produced goods. Then, they began exporting to other Asian countries and exporting price-competitive goods to the US and Europe. And finally, they mounted full brand-driven global marketing campaigns. The powerful market position that Lexus has built in the US in the teeth of such rivals as Mercedes-Benz, BMW and Cadillac is one dramatic example of the triumph of Big M, little m Marketing, as is the fact that Toyota is now the world's 12th most valuable brand.

As a domestic market, Japan is both the most homogeneous (with a single language and relatively small geographic spread) and also one of the most diverse and complex markets in Asia, due to its massive size (the third largest single market in the world) and status as originator of trends and products that have influence around the region, and increasingly, around the world. Japanese marketers today are some of the Asia region's most creative and proactive BIG M, little m Marketers, both in their home market, and abroad. For international marketers, the power of "Japan Inc." as a marketing force is immediately felt, both in the form of active assistance the Japanese government provides for their firms abroad, and for the domestic protection the Ministry of International Trade and Industry provides these firms in Japan.

Many of Japan's innovations and opportunities come from situations unique to the Japanese market. For example, Sony invented the Walkman as a way of listening to music (founder Akio Morita's favorite was classical) without disturbing other commuters on the way to work. The personal listening device was created to promote harmony with the listener's outside world, rather than the conflict of imposing one person's tastes on another.

Other attributes, such as the importance of collective success over individual success and other traditional social-cultural values unique to Japan, pervade the marketing environment. Despite international success and interchange, nationalism ("We Japanese") and compatibility with traditional values are still components of marketing success. Younger people are more likely than older groups to try foreign products. Interest in imported products and international brands is primarily fueled by imitation (as with the Chinese) and has built a strong market for overseas fashion, luxury goods, and technologically sophisticated products from Europe and the US.

Korea

As already noted, thanks to offering innovation and good value for money, Korean brands such as Samsung have made powerful inroads to Western markets, and there are hundreds of other *chaebol* conglomerate companies and entrepreneurial ventures in Korea set to follow the same course.

Korea's drive to rival and surpass Japan remains a force for that country's international economic development, and Korea is likely to be among the next Asian leaders in Big M, little m Marketing. The country is well positioned to be a direct competitor of Japan in Mainland China. Following the "Japan Inc." model, this influence can be extended worldwide. For this to happen, however, Korea will need to continue to work to resolve its internal political/economic conflicts. The tremendous amount of energy and attention paid to modernizing Korean firms and resolving labor issues is profoundly distracting from the quest to develop globally relevant brands.

China

The future international prospects for China come into sharp focus in light of the fact that different parts of China are tied economically to other parts of the world. For example, the links from Guangzhou to Hong Kong, Malaysia, Indonesia and the US; Shanghai to Japan and Singapore; Xiamin to Taiwan; Jilin to both Koreas and Russia. These relationships hinge primarily on China as a low-cost manufacturing center (exports), or on the supply of technology or goods not currently available in China (imports). In both cases, the role of overseas Chinese business people is important in the development of BIG M Marketing, in that mainland Chinese businesses are able to interact with people educated overseas and exposed to the dynamics of free market economies. The ideas brought into China by the overseas Chinese, matched with market-oriented reforms, are powerful drivers of BIG M Marketing.

This will not be an immediate or swift process, however, as there are entrenched Chinese institutions that influence marketing practices. Family connections to the communist party are almost unbreakable links in control of the supply chain, with a social network of friends also forming the backbone of the business community. Government officials are committed *"status quo"* consumers, and unlikely any time soon to experiment with new ways of doing business or purchasing brands. This group wants to avoid risks of all sorts, and free market competition is certainly threatening.

There is hidden marketing potential in China because even though the average family income is less than US$700 per year, that family actually has higher disposable income than might be expected because expenses for many of their basic necessities such as housing and utilities are subsidized by the government. As an example, only 10% of Chinese households have hot running water, but 80% own televisions.

The opportunities are also burgeoning for B2B and infrastructure marketing. For example, China is projected to need 600-800 more passenger jets over the next 15 years to meet the demands of 18% annual growth, and will spend around US$60 billion to meet the demand.

AFTA

As a trading block, the ASEAN nations (Thailand, Brunei, Malaysia, Singapore, The Philippines, Vietnam and Indonesia) have the potential to exceed North American Free Trade Agreement (NAFTA). Their planned regional free trade area is called ASEAN Free Trade Area (AFTA) and covers a total market of 400 million people. One challenge will be for these amalgamated countries to coordinate their export efforts with a sufficient amount of Big M Marketing muscle to rival Japanese, US, and European brands around Asia and the world. Jollibee Food is looking to expand their fast-food franchise beyond their home market of the Philippines, and carve out a niche in the international restaurant business. And perhaps Malaysia's Proton automobile brand has the power to become a regional or global player, though currently the focus is on keeping the Malaysian automobile industry nationalized, rather than driving international expansion.

India

India has a major BIG M role to play in Asia, with a tremendous reserve of a talented and well-educated labor pool. Perhaps the most apparent "first wave" of Indian influence in Asia is the outsourcing of business processes to Indian firms by Asia-based companies and multinationals in the region. Referring back to the "Japan Inc." model, the domestic Indian market is so large and filled with so much potential that it is likely India will remain in the internally focused phase of its development of Big M strategic marketing. By the time it needs or wants to look at international expansion, the markets may have become saturated with brands, leaving price competitiveness as the only benefit on which to compete.

As the world economy grows there will be room for several new regional powerhouses to meet demand within Asia, and also to drive exports and deliver the next generation of global brands. In addition to the myriad macro economic factors such as the WTO, access to capital, and investment education, the development of BIG M, little m Marketing will be an essential part of this region's efforts to enhance its global competitive advantage.

Eight Signposts To Success

"What is the use of running when you are on the wrong road?"

- Proverb

6

Eight Signposts To Success

BIG M, little m Marketing may be guided by a Compass and a Map, but as with any journey, it is often the signposts along the way that provide the most immediate and clear direction, as well as a clear indication of whether you are even on the right road or not. This section of the book provides Eight Signposts to Success – guiding principles that show the way forward – illustrated with real life examples of companies that have traveled this way before. Their experience, including both the BIG M strategic approach taken and the specific little m tactics used, can help point you along the right marketing course.

The Signposts to Success are not scientific theories or hard-and-fast rules, but rather common-sense guidelines that allow individual practitioners to make their own way. BIG M, little m Marketing is a pragmatic mixture of "in-the-field" experience, inspiration from international best practice, and anecdotal wisdom appropriate to local market economic and cultural conditions. Each of the following eight sections outlines one of the BIG M, little m Marketing Signposts, and is headed up by one or two quotations based on the idea that often the most sophisticated marketing theories can be derived from or boiled down to a homespun maxim.

- **EAT THE ELEPHANT ONE BITE AT A TIME**

Conceiving the right marketing strategy and meshing it with perfectly selected and implemented tactics is an elephant-sized job. And like eating an elephant, it is really only possible when tackled in small increments. And ... as with any big task, start now because it will take you a lot longer than you think. The market is not standing still and neither should you.

- **UNDER PROMISE AND OVER DELIVER**

The promise of a perfect strategy can be wrecked by unrealistically raised and unmet expectations. Similarly, over-ambitious marketing tactics can drag you into a nightmare of logistics and detail that can never yield enough results to justify the expenditure of money and time. Carefully assess the market and your company's capability, and design campaigns that delight your customers against reasonable expectations.

- **EMBRACE YOUR WEAKNESSES**

Any worthy competitor is going to analyze and attack your company's weaknesses, so get there first, and design marketing strategies that either make your weaknesses irrelevant, or use them for competitive advantage. If your company's success relies on your weakest skill, change your strategy.

- **THE VISION THING**

Worldwide, the value of mission statements and corporate visions is vastly overrated, and many Asia companies have either drafted paragraphs that are nothing more than a description of what they do, or worse, crafted ambitious prose describing business dreams that would never materialize. However, an electrifying, ambitious marketing strategy can be a powerful motivator for your team, and help define your market position against your competitors. The personal charisma and "evangelical" fervor of the senior management team are also important factors in a company's advancement, and cannot be quantified, except perhaps as invaluable.

- **MOVE UPSTREAM**

Moving marketing upstream means getting marketing matters moved up higher in the decision-making process. Go to the CEO with a great marketing idea, not to the marketing manager. Work with the people who formulate and agree on strategy, not just those who sign off on tactical plans and budgets. Write your company's marketing plan at the same time as the business plan, not as an administrative afterthought. Moving upstream can also mean pushing several stages up the supply chain and creating an innovation that eliminates or replaces unnecessary or low value-added steps, or going directly to government officials to liberalize regulations that are obstructing your growth.

- **GO, GO, GO!**

Particularly in undeveloped or rapidly changing markets, the marketer with a predilection to action is rewarded. Set your BIG M strategy. Move fast. Push forward. Make mistakes. Learn. Succeed. And then do more of what meets customer needs, profitably. Management textbooks on marketing have their place, but so too does luck. When you "go, go, go" the law of averages means that you have more opportunities to make you own luck, and if you have either your BIG M or little m marketer wrong, at least you'll have more data points to work from and will know faster.

- **IT'S THE CUSTOMER, STUPID**

The customers are in control and you are not. It's a conversation, not a monologue. We all know that's true, but how can you, the manager, force yourself and your organisation to "feel the pain" and respond with specific, actionable new customer-oriented systems and structures? You will either have to use customer research as a "big stick" to force management change, or set out to create a sub-culture within your organisation to redirect focus back to the customer. Either way works; one or the other is essential.

- **STEAL THE WHEEL!**

When it comes to management and marketing technique, no two situations are exactly the same, so the wise marketer does not need to reinvent the wheel, but steal it. Does that mean it is OK to copy intellectual property? No, certainly not. However, liberally borrowing from other people's marketing strategies is fine, especially when you are in a different industry or a different part of the world and you are inspired by the approach, rather than simply lifting the campaign idea. Spend as much management energy as possible on orchestrating strategy and tactics, rather than on unharnessed creativity or fruitless reinvention of the wheel.

The art of BIG M, little m Marketing is built up from a constant intermingling and reiteration of these approaches to marketing problems. Pick the guiding principle that seems most appropriate for the challenge you are tackling, or just browse through the list and look for inspiration wherever you find it.

EAT THE ELEPHANT ONE BITE AT A TIME

"Ice frozen as deep as three chi does not happen in one cold day."
- Chinese proverb

Building a marketing strategy and meshing it harmoniously with your tactics is not a fast, one-step process. If you set out to eat an elephant in a single day, you would fail unless a small village of hungry friends joined you. The only way is one bite at a time, and then the seemingly impossible comes within reach. It is also an iterative process, in which each day new possibilities open up and more mistakes are made and rectified. Business people are often lead astray by the notion that, "What the mind can conceive, then man can achieve", and assume that with hard work and diligence they can make their strategies work. The reality is that no matter how good your strategy, it will have to evolve and change as you respond to:

- feedback from the market as to what works and what doesn't;
- changing market conditions;
- competitive moves;
- successes and failures of your marketing tactics; and the professional skills of your senior executives.

Over time, your strategy will shift to more closely fit with the skills that your company has mastered. Sometimes learning new skills (and adopting new tactics to meet the needs of a brilliant strategy) is more difficult and less economical than tweaking your strategy. Similarly, companies that drift from their core competencies often find that having the right strategy is not protection against disaster.

Determine one course and steer by it

The first marketing decisions you must make are to determine what core business you are in, who your customers are, what they want, and how you can deliver it better (e.g. faster delivery; cheaper than competitors; better customer service) than anyone in the business. When you are clear about your own BIG M business strategy, you have taken the first step of your BIG M and little m Marketing journey.

General Electric (GE) has worked hard to match its company strategy with its ability to execute in each of its many disparate businesses from jet engines to medical equipment to consumer electronics to financial services. GE selects high-growth, potentially high-yield businesses and then manages them as well as possible. The key to this strategy is the use of growth/return criteria to select which businesses belong in the portfolio, rather than making decisions purely based along rigid industry sector lines. GE has sustained this approach for many years, by continually dropping the lowest performing 10% of every division's staff annually, and selling any businesses that were not number one or two in their sector. By being single-minded about this financial performance based strategy and "eating the elephant one bite at a time" (case-by-case, year-by-year, employee-by-employee) the company has generated many quarters of profit.

Years ago, Pepsico faced a similar need to define its portfolio of businesses. Management had diversified away from just soft drinks by acquiring companies such as United Van Lines, Wilson Sporting Goods, and Pizza Hut. Watching shareholder value lag, the company decided to focus on soft drinks, snack foods and quick-service restaurants, and divest the other companies. Later, with the spin-off of the restaurant division comprising Pizza Hut, Taco Bell and KFC into what at the time was called Tricon (now Yum! Brands,Inc.), Pepsico switched focus exclusively to soft drinks and snack foods. These product ranges share similar end consumers and distribution chains and marketing learning.

GE and Pepsico have chosen different ways to define their core businesses. However, the result is the same. They both align their marketing strategies and tactics and match clear and consistent management direction with a portfolio of brand names, products and management methods that can be rolled out globally. So what can you the manager do to bring your strategies and tactics closer together on a consistent and steady timetable?

Innovate by the stopwatch; assess by the calendar

To eat the elephant, start right now! Look for opportunities to tweak strategies and revamp tactics on a day-to-day basis. Don't wait until your annual planning cycle begins; small incremental gains as soon as possible will aggregate into considerable improvements over time. There is no need to continuously assess what you are doing; just keep going with your program and evaluate quarterly what works and what doesn't. Get into the discipline of "innovating by the stopwatch and assessing by the calendar" to keep the process loose and fluid, with ideas sparking off without rigid rules.

This practice is well-rewarded especially in price-sensitive markets such as consumer electronics, in which millions of dollars are invested in research, product development and manufacturing. There is a small time window during which the product can be marketed at a premium price. If a company finds it has stumbled onto a winning formula of product, design and functionality, then product shortages are likely and prices will stay correspondingly high. However well designed the product may be, if sales start off slowly, inventories will rise, prices will have to be dropped to drive demand and distributors and retailers may demand additional incentives or discounts. These decisions must be made immediately. Every product has only one life cycle, and if it is rapidly going from launch to dead stock, marketers must pull out every little m Marketing tactic up their sleeves to prolong the cycle and give the product a chance to catch the public's favor.

The time for action is now; the time to assess is at the end of the quarter. Aggressive little m Marketing can drive enough sales to keep the product on the shelves. Changing market trends demand a new BIG M Marketing strategy *now* to position the product for success. Most of this day-by-day analysis needs to be as quick as a reflex, based on market knowledge and experience. For example, every time a new audio or video format (cassette, CD, Super Audio CD, DAC, DAT, Minidisc, DVD, MP3) is released, it starts as a premium audiophile and/or wealthy "early-adopter" product. Within just a few years, the new format either has full saturation in the market, or has failed to catch on. The format that initially had pride-of-place in the living room super hi-fi system soon becomes available in car audio, then portable players and before you know it, your kids are using it in the playroom and the cycle begins again. The reaction times in this business are so fast that proper assessment can often only occur after the game is over and the market has already picked the winners and losers.

In this respect, Volkswagen (VW) has done a brilliant job marketing the Beetle. From its origins before World War II as a people's car (literally *volks wagen*), the Beetle was by its definition cheap and for everyone. With the introduction of the new Beetle in 1998, however, it was positioned as a thoroughly modern, stylish vehicle. There were playful references back to the earlier Beetle, but in its styling, colours, performance and price, it was a different breed of bug. Even as sales rise, VW has kept the scarce/sought-after image and positioning in place. If the whim of fickle car buyers had shifted subtly so the Beetle's design no longer appealed, or if a sudden worldwide recession had made cost a major consideration, then the BIG M strategy would have had to have been changed, along with the need for substantial discounts and dealer incentives. To sell a car with a heritage of being cheap and accessible as being rare and highly valued was a calculated risk. As it was, VW has stayed the course and built a lengthened and sustainable product life cycle.

Be ruthless about continuous improvement

No company ever shrank to greatness; but make it a regular part of management discipline to cut off the bottom 10% of your marketing activities and budget every quarter, and replace them with a new 10% of better and stronger ideas, or at least experimental campaigns that test new market realities and opportunities. Even if a campaign is considered to be yielding reasonable returns, lop it off if it falls in the bottom 10% of your overall program and reapply the funds toward potentially more effective strategies or tactics. The new campaigns may work better or worse, but the discipline assures that there are always fresh funds available for new promising ideas, and the marketing budgets do not become arthritic.

When you are doing your marketing by "Eating the elephant one bite at a time," absolutely no part of your marketing activities PR budget can be taken for granted. Every item must be scrutinized and measured. If it is adding value, an activity should be kept or expanded with additional budget support. Often little m Marketing budgets follow the "80-for-20" rule, whereby 20% of the marketing expenditure is delivering 80% of the return. This situation can yield efficiencies, especially if you are continually cutting from the bottom. However, if the bulk of your sales or profit is being delivered by one or just a few marketing initiatives, then you are in trouble if the market or competitive landscape shifts and makes these revenue drivers obsolete. To some extent, formulating strategy is a leap of faith, and one must be sure to be continuously allocated funds to BIG M marketing strategy activities such as research, test marketing and new product development, even if the "one bite at a time" payback doesn't seem to justify the expenditure. Allocating 10% of your marketing budget to pure BIG M activities is prudent, especially if you have the discipline to continuously review, revamp, and reject the activities in your budget.

Avoid "Boom/Splat" marketing

In the late 1960s it was The Beatles and love beads. In the late 1970s it was flared pants and lava lamps. In the late 1980s it was disco and "greed is good." And the late 1990s were marked by overblown orgiastic website launch parties and expensive, quirky dotcom TV and magazine ad campaigns.

Thinking back to those bygone days (was it really just a few years ago?) it requires a bit of effort to remember the logic of "front loading" all your marketing activities into a giant mushroom cloud of frenetic activity. Celebrity endorsements. Ads on every hilltop and bus side. Massive parties. A news release every day or two. And all backed up by millions of SPAM e-mails.

In 1999, these conversations could be heard all over Asia ... and all over the world. "Heh, we've got first-mover advantage ... We've got to win the land grab in our space ... If we build it they will come ... Only the top two sites in any category will get any funding ... The Internet has changed all the rules and we will continue to grow at 8,000% a year." And why not? The money, drive, promises, and predictions were there – all signed and authenticated. Microsoft, eBay, and Amazon.com (amongst others) were living proof that it would all work, and make you a billionaire in the process.

The immense, intense marketing drives that went into launching new and wonderful dotcoms were full of sound and fury, and launched companies high into orbit with the belief that there they would stay, circling the globe with millions looking up in wonder. However, gravity, in more cases than not, proved to be too strong, dragging them back down through the atmosphere with their burn rates sparkling dramatically behind.

The quality of the service and technology would market itself – if we build it, they will come. Just get the name out there once, and the rest will follow. Boom … splat. BIG M Marketing at its worst. All the strategy and all the tactics crammed into a very short time frame. And then, silence.

Consumer audiences and their expectations have changed, and now a direct-mail letter is simply not enough to create a buzz. The Internet also means that anyone and everyone is a writer, a critic, an editor, and a publisher. The barriers have been torn down and we are left with a billion voices all wanting to tell you their opinion.

So what's the answer? Although the "boom" may be good, it's the "splat" that is not. One of many lessons of the dotcom era is to plan your marketing consistently over time. Sure, build in highs for product launches and roaring stock markets. But also build in rest times and continuity campaigns that hold customers once they are hooked.

BIG M Marketing campaigns require the three S's - Subtlety, Strategy and Sustainability

Subtlety – Dare to be subtle; be clear and plain speaking, but don't always go for the obvious. How many times have you seen the phrase "Our revolutionary technology is pioneering a new era for the next millennium"? Forget it. It's consistent innovation that sticks in the mind.

Strategy – Make your company or brand credible and distinct. Technology goes out of date in months, but brands last. Tailor your BIG M Marketing campaign for your business model and target market. There *are* "off-the-rack" strategies (such as the ones in the Navigation Tools section of this book), but even the best ones require customization.

Sustainability – After any big noise, there is an echo and then silence. As part of your BIG M Marketing you should plan to build your brand and get your name out there periodically, but save the dollars for the consistent little m Marketing that will drive sales and bring a real return on investment.

"Eating the elephant one bite at a time" has two profound implications for the way you conduct your marketing. First, your little m Marketing must begin immediately, be relentless, and adapt constantly to assure that your campaign is in tune with the markets. Innovation is highlighted as a trait of industry winners, but in fact it is often the hallmark first and foremost of survivors. Second, BIG M Marketing requires you to think about strategy in the broadest possible way. Every day, in every small way, you are presented with opportunities for competitive advantage, from selecting the right people for the right positions, to pricing, to locating retail locations, and the list goes on and on. Any one of these decisions in isolation might not be the tipping point, but taken together, they are critical and require constant vigilance and management attention.

Under Promise and Over Deliver

"Be careful what you wish for ... you may get it."

- Anonymous

"Unhappiness is best defined as the difference between our talents and our expectations."

- Edward de Bono

If the goal of doing marketing well is to not just meet but also to beat customers' expectations, then 90% of the battle is making sure that expectations are set at the right level to begin with. Perhaps the largest stumbling block to effective BIG M, little m Marketing is that management sets strategies that generate very high expectations that can rarely be met in actual execution. A clever strategy is one that sets customer expectations at relatively low levels, and then delights. The same result delivered can either be a triumph or a disaster, depending on what the customer was led to believe would happen.

Set reasonable expectations

An excellent example of setting customer expectations properly is the tear-away success of NTT DoCoMo's i-mode service, which enables users to access the Internet and send and receive e-mail over a mobile phone. Thanks to a good start provided by the company's previous monopoly status, and bolstered by hot services such as i-mode, around 60% of Japan's 57 million mobile-phone subscribers use one of NTT DoCoMo's products. The mobile Internet experience i-mode provides is truly revolutionary, but the features and consumer benefits of the service are not the primary reasons for its success.

In Japan, Internet access has until recently been expensive and difficult to arrange. The dial-up Internet services charge relatively high fees compared to other markets, and the fixed phone lines required are also expensive and take time to order. Then, along comes i-mode. Suddenly, you don't need a fixed line to access the Internet. You don't need a PC. The cost-effective, easy access to the Internet and e-mail exceeded customers' expectations and helped make it a hit service. The selling points of the i-mode service are its "mobility and connectivity." Customers would have been disappointed if the main selling point was the quality of the Internet experience, because compared to home-based services, access is slow and limited, and the tiny phone keys require seemingly endless rapid pushing to compose even the most basic message.

However, many Japanese workers and students have long commutes everyday on public transport, and the quiet, private, entertaining i-mode experience has given them something to do with their down time. i-mode's experience competes well with other potential uses of people's time such as reading the newspaper or studying work documents.

Now as NTT DoCoMo rolls out its third generation service from its Tokyo starting point, it will be interesting to see if consumers (such as *oyayubizoku* "clan of the thumbs," and the "paka-paka girls" known for the sound their phone cases make as they flip open and shut) remain satisfied with the experience as their expectations are raised. In some markets, 3G has been said to stand for games, girls, and gambling due to the most popular uses of the mobile Internet. So far, i-mode has done a good job of under promising and over delivering to the Japanese consumer.

Taking up residence online

Another example of a company that set and exceeded customer expectations is Colliers Jardine. The property company had a Website from the earliest days of the World Wide Web, primarily providing basic corporate and contact information. In 2000, the company's international residential property division set out to use the power of the Internet to help property buyers find their dream home for living or investment online. From the very start of the project, the company realized it had three core strengths:

- A deep understanding of the residential property market.
- A database of interested customers and prospects.
- An attractive listing of international properties.

The Hong Kong-based team in charge resisted the dotcom era temptation to rip up everything they knew and start afresh on the Web. In addition, Colliers Jardine runs a highly successful business using a wide range of "old-economy" tools such as postcards to clients via mail, newspaper ads, property exhibitions with building models at five-star hotels, and other methods of personal contact with a relatively wealthy and well defined target group of interested potential buyers. There was little need to radically switch to a new business model, and there was some conservative but prudent management resistance toward over-emphasizing the online component when the off-line was working so well. As part of the overall mandate to match buyers and sellers, the Internet is an effective tool and way to efficiently share information about properties worldwide.

Colliers Jardine launched their international residential property website (www.residential.colliers.com) under the theme of a "world of property online." The online component of their business was presented to customers and prospects as a useful tool to review property listed with Colliers Jardine worldwide, rather than a major revolution in the property sales industry. Although the database of available properties, presentation and features put the website at the front of the property industry game, the company underplayed the benefits of the website and simply positioned it as a comprehensive, easy-to-access catalog of its property listings.

By under promising and over delivering, Colliers Jardine and their customers were able to get their customers and potential customers immediate and in-depth access to their real estate listings. In addition, they were able to take advantage of these benefits without re-inventing the company as a "dotcom" company by branding their on-line presence in a way that was closely in tune with the rest of their business. Clients and prospects did not feel that the company had moved into a new business, and Colliers Jardine harnessed the technology without losing business focus, or experiencing the downside of being too closely aligned with the passing Internet bubble.

Following are some specific strategies to help make sure your BIG M Marketing strategy does not make promises your little m Marketing can't keep.

Make small promises and keep them quickly

There is real danger in making big promises to your customers and then setting long deadlines and outlining complicated processes before they can be met. Of course you should be ambitious in your BIG M Marketing objectives, but you do not have to share your entire vision with everybody right away. Often it is better to divide the larger task into incremental steps (Eating the Elephant One Bite at a Time) and make a series of smaller, easier to keep promises.

An example of how this can go wrong was illustrated by an Asia-based company that made a far-reaching deal to market its product across all the communications of a media powerhouse, ranging from the Internet, to TV, to print publications. In reality, the massive size and scope of the project was far beyond the little m Marketing capabilities of the company. They could not execute, and juggled multiple deadlines around the region, with no dedicated marketing staff to make good on all the promises that had been made. The execution of the campaign was eventually delegated to the company's joint venture partners in each country, despite the fact that the media giant's properties were regional.

The promise of the regional BIG M Marketing idea remained bright until one day when the managing director of the company was flying home and picked up a copy at the airport of one of the magazines involved. Inside was a double page spread ad for the product – but it was in tiny type in terrible English. One of the joint venture partners had put it in without having central headquarters review it, and since they had been in a hurry, they raced to meet the deadline with an ad that fell way, way short of the promise. The over promising and under delivering put the entire image and positioning of the company at risk, and was a phenomenal waste of staff time, working on a project they could not complete.

The same group could have had a happier conclusion from this experience if they had simply committed to a few magazine ads in one of the regional publications and hired a competent advertising agency to create and produce the ads. The sweeping vision of the cross-media BIG M marketing campaign would have been missed, but the little m Marketing goal of useful ads in targeted publications could have been accomplished. A few small promises made and kept quickly builds trust and marketing momentum more than grand, vague promises.

Blow the whistle on yourself when you get it wrong

Another operational rule of under promising and over delivering is to be the first one to blow the whistle and point out a shortfall, even if (especially if) you were the one responsible. BIG M, little m Marketing at its best is an objective process, freed from personal opinions and political agendas. A passionate belief in the right way forward is not enough; confusing your commitment with actually getting results is a dead end. You must strive to objectify the marketing situation, keep a clear head, and not allow your opinions or relationship with your colleagues to cloud your judgment. When a campaign isn't working, be the first to suggest pulling the plug.

A different angle on under promising and over delivering is being the first to say that your campaign is under delivering, then your integrity and credibility will remain intact for the next time you need to make a promise.

The Acer Group of Taiwan built a solid reputation as an Asia-based computer hardware brand. Acer is a good example of how a company found that it had over-diversified and perhaps lost its way, and is now refocusing on a new strategy to guide its business forward, based as much on what the company would STOP doing as what it would START doing. In 2000, the company suffered a US$135million operating loss, a disastrous plant fire and dipping share prices. The company needed to make some bold moves to stay financially viable.

Stan Shih, Acer's founder and CEO, who had previously delegated day-to-day management, stepped back into a hands-on role. His conclusion: "The issue is focus," and he identified that the problem was Acer tried to do too much. Acer makes and sells products with the Acer brand that sometimes competed with the products it makes for other global companies. These Original Equipment Manufacturer (OEM) contracts were subsidizing the losses of Acer's own brand products. This business increased overall sales, but made companies wary of having Acer manufacture their machines for fear they would be subsidizing their own competition and also sharing technology secrets with a competitor.

Mr. Shih took the decision to completely separate the Acer brand sales business from the manufacturing business and to refocus the Acer business on services. The manufacturing group has been spun off entirely into an entity called Wistron that is expected to be sold. Acer Communications & Multimedia, an autonomous unit for over 10 years, emerged with the new name Benq in December 2001. Benq is an effort to distance Acer's consumer-focused communications and multimedia sectors from the Acer name.

The move away from the company's previous efforts to be perceived primarily as a branded hardware manufacturer and marketer is a bold one. Acer is staking the company's future on its ability to create a new globally recognized services brand, while leveraging existing relationships, local knowledge and cost-efficient ways of doing business. Mr Shih reinforces the continuity of the old strategy with the new one, saying, "When we were founded 25 years ago, we were a service company, so services are a part of our history."

The jury is still out as to whether this bold BIG M strategy is a success, but this "jump shift" in business focus and long-term vision required considerable commitment and BIG M Marketing foresight by Acer as a corporation, as well as strong personal leadership by Stan Shih. By having the courage to see that the current BIG M strategy was not working in the marketplace and deciding on a new direction, Acer may have gained a new lease on life.

Have no fear

The expression "Who dares wins" is a good motto for gutsy makers of big promises. Whether or not you are ultimately successful, if you are afraid or show any hint of an inability to deliver on your promises, then your efforts will be doomed.

A courageous example is Sondhi Limthongkul, the Thailand-based media baron who aspired to launch a truly pan-Asian media group with the ambitious regional newspaper *Asia Times*, and an array of satellite TV and other media ventures. Starting in 1995, his M Group holding company put US$20 million into launching *Asia Times*. He told the editorial staff, "Don't worry about the money. I have long pockets.." The newspaper folded not long after, during the 1997 Asia economic downturn amid difficulties in securing sufficient advertising to make the publication viable. If the advertising markets had been different, or if he had made a succession of smaller-scale promises, he may have reached his goal, but none can question his vision and fortitude to make such a big promise. The net effect, however, was over promising and under delivering.

Whether dealing with B2B trade customers or directly with consumers on the street, the BIG M, little m Marketer will always be well served to make smaller promises and deliver bigger results any day. Make it your mantra: under promise and over deliver.

Embrace Your Weaknesses

"Real knowledge is to know the extent of one's ignorance."
- Confucius

"When there is turmoil under the heavens, little problems are dealt with as if they were big problems and big problems are not dealt with at all. When there is order under the heavens, big problems are reduced to smaller problems and smaller problems should not obsess us."
- Chinese proverb, relayed to Henry Kissinger by Lee Kuan Yew, Senior Minister of Singapore.

Your competitor will identify and attack your weak points intensively. It is human nature to try to bury one's weaknesses and focus on one's strengths. A critical component of BIG M, little m Marketing is to understand your own weaknesses better than your adversary and wherever possible use them to your advantage. Recognizing one's own weaknesses is not something that one does naturally, and more often than not, it is not something that individuals or companies do publicly.

Kick boxing clever

The parallels between martial arts and marketing have been drawn before. For example, *Aikido* is a Japanese martial art that focuses not on punching or kicking opponents, but rather on using one's energy to gain control over them, or to throw them away from you. It is not a static art, and places emphasis on motion and the dynamics of movement. The idea is not to hurt your opponent if you can help it – after all, your opponent has only attacked you so that you may improve your technique.

The same is true for BIG M, little m Marketing. The best approach is often to turn the strength of the forces marshalled against us to our advantage. A clever example of this comes from VTech, the Hong Kong-based maker of consumer electronics and toys. VTech markets an impressive array of learning toys for children, based on computer chips that are outdated by today's brutal pace of change in the semiconductor industry. However, VTech has outfitted chips from previous generations of technology into low-tech sectors such as toys, and found new life for them through smart positioning and marketing. For example, computer chips that just 20 years ago would have rivalled the computing power found in governments and universities are now used to control talking dolls or spelling tutorial devices.

With economies of scale in chip manufacture, and Moore's law (the computing power of integrated circuits will double approximately every 18 months), VTech can specify increasingly powerful and intelligent chips in lower and lower cost and day-to-day applications that previously never could have justified such computing power.

This trend, however, is a double-edged sword for manufacturers and marketers. In the US, for example, the decrease in chip prices and increase in available computing power has driven the penetration of PCs. As a result, more and more families with higher disposable income are not buying their younger children toy computers first and then upgrading them to real PCs later. Instead, they are either buying young children PC's of their own, or they are passing along their perfectly serviceable PC components to their kids as they upgrade to a new processor, more memory, or a flat screen.

Initially, this trend presented a real threat to VTech and appeared to be a weakness in their competitive position. However, they embraced their role in the market as the "cheaper alternative to a real PC" and targeted lower-income families who may not have the disposable income to give their children full-function models at an early age, but who want to give them a computer-driven learning opportunity. By embracing previous generation technology, VTech has secured and built market share in a very competitive sector. This strategy almost misfired with VTech's purchase of AT&T's telephone manufacturing division, but the issues were more to do with an unexpected amount of inventory, rather than a miscalculation of the value of existing technology. VTech moved on after the purchase to market the phones as inexpensive units for home use, and also added colours and styles that gave new lifestyle interest to existing models.

Tell time by the stopped clock

There is an old riddle: Which clock tells the correct time most often? A clock that runs five minutes slow each hour? A clock that runs five minutes fast each hour? A clock that has stopped? The answer is the clock that has stopped tells the correct time the most often: twice a day as the correct time matches the stopped hands. The learning for BIG M, little m Marketers from this riddle is do not be so eager to catch the trend or cut your losses if the market is not going your way that you miss the "slow-burn" opportunities.

Executives raised in the dotcom era are used to making immediate decisions based on limited facts and under extreme time and financial pressure. You cast the dice. You win. You lose. Another generation of marketer (who may shortly reappear on the Asia scene) "tells time by the stopped clock," and is not willing to trade in steady, if somewhat plodding, growth for short-term spikes in the sales curve that cause the entire organisation – from marketing to sales to manufacturing – stress as they struggle to meet deadlines and quotas.

As an example of "steady as she goes" marketing, the herbal ointment Tiger Balm is probably Asia's best. The salve contains no tiger, and is a centuries-old generic concoction, but even today it has a loyal following of consumers.

The leaping tiger symbol, the small hexagonal jars, and paper boxes are a BIG M branding idea. Adorned by a tiger jumping across the label, Tiger Balm still has continuing, broad, compelling appeal to new, more modern target audiences. Named after one of the founder's sons, Boon Haw (gentle tiger), Tiger Balm made a fortune for the Haw Par Corporation, which plowed part of its proceeds back into highly visible community charity projects, further strengthening its brand.

There is no major secret to Tiger Balm's success: just strong and consistent little m Marketing execution. A readily identifiable product (name and packaging) backed up by consistent product quality and satisfied users have kept the brand alive in an increasingly turbulent market. Like the stopped clock, Tiger Balm gets it right more often than most other brands that are constantly changing their strategies and trying new positionings.

Another Asian brand on the world stage has taken a different course. Red Bull, which at home in Thailand is primarily an energy tonic for people wanting to stay alert, is now gaining sales and visibility overseas as a high-powered drinks mixer on the club scene in Europe and the US. This trendy and "of the moment" positioning has given the brand a tremendous boost via its international distributors. The product formulation used overseas is different to the one used in Thailand, although the branding is the same. Tiger Balm has remained true to its roots and has held on to the same positioning it started with. Will Red Bull's new, hip incarnation give it an opportunity to push on to be a lasting, globally recognized brand, or will it drop out of fashion like a plummeting song on the pop charts? The BIG M decision to change the positioning and the formulation has been made, and it will be interesting to see over the next few years whether it will prove wiser to "tell time by the stopped clock" like Tiger Balm, or accelerate into the hyper world of international marketing trends like Red Bull.

See yourself as others see you

It is a wise marketer who uses research; it is a fool who is ruled by it. Research is a critical tool in helping marketers identify their own weaknesses (in a relatively private environment) before others discover and exploit them. The BIG M Marketing strategic power of understanding your company's true place in the eye and heart of your customer - and that of your competitor - is awesome. Use research to discover your own weaknesses before you invest in expensive marketing programs that may flop. Experience is a costly and public way to learn many of the same lessons that research can teach. Conversely, a very real and tempting danger is to be ruled by the research results. Research can only identify the current perceptions and facts and what customers think they want. On the other hand, BIG M Marketing often requires marketers to actually anticipate customer needs; they do not have the luxury of the classic marketing paradigm of first giving customers what they want, then giving them what they need.

A high-risk marketing strategy is for a company to immediately jump to a conclusion about what they believe their customers will need, despite whatever short-term weaknesses they may have identified. For the more prudent, the use of research allows companies a private-eye look into the marketing environment that can minimize their risk, and encourage them to boldly step out with a BIG M Marketing initiative that shifts the marketing rules in their industry sector. If the research effort identifies weaknesses, it's far better to know about them and address them in advance.

Whether through the use of research, common sense or internal management findings such as a SWOT (strengths, weaknesses, opportunities, threats) analysis, the savvy BIG M, little m Marketing practitioner will embrace his/her weaknesses, and learn to work with and around them.

The Vision Thing

"It is undesirable and limiting to be like a frog in a well. A broad, open-minded worldview is far more enriching."

- Korean proverb

"The Vision Thing," as GE's Jack Welsh called it, is far from being an empty touchy-feely exercise in corporate communications; it is a highly practical tool in the BIG M, little m Marketing toolbox.

Steven Covey, author of *Seven Habits of Highly Effective People,* is just one of dozens of very influential thinkers who helped business people during the 1980s and early 1990s become aware of the importance of having a clear vision of where they want their companies and their own careers to be heading. The movement helped operationally-focused managers to learn to lift their heads and realize that much of business success and leadership is about setting clear goals and making sure the whole team buys into the sense of purpose and mission required to reach those goals.

Since that time, the value of mission statements and corporate visions has become overrated and the process of developing them has taken up far too much executive time in workshops and weekend retreats. Corporate visions are a bit like finding the love of your life … if you have to try too hard, it's probably not right. A clear statement of your business purpose is now considered necessary to run a business, in much the same category as health plans or water coolers.

A vision statement is not just a literal description of your business and objectives, but neither should it be so vague or poetical that it bears little resemblance to the reality of your business. Be bold and set high targets, but not to the extent that your goals are un-credible or unrealistic. Often the best vision statements come from the company founders or senior executives who are able to articulate the bigger reasons why they get out of bed every morning and come to work. Whether delivered like inspiration, or carefully crafted by a group of senior executives, the right vision statement can be a battle flag for all the troops to follow.

Do a few things right

If the vision for a particular firm is "Be all things to all people 24 hours a day everywhere," then there is no way you would believe it. You wouldn't trust the company as a supplier, as a customer, and you certainly wouldn't be an investor. In Asia, however, the vision has been to use the company's networks and contacts to maximize any type of possible business, even if it is out of the firm's area of core competency. On the other hand, listed companies face tremendous pressure from both private shareholders and retail investors to diversify their revenue streams and to broaden their base of business (by product, geography or industry type). With these pressures to diversify, firms often forget to "do a few things right."

Whatever risks the BIG M Marketing strategy may bring with it, it is certainly a clear, focused vision for the future that can be easily understood by:

- customers
- shareholders
- regulators
- vendors
- employees.

Top down or bottom up?

Where does the inspiration for BIG M Marketing vision come from? It can come from the company's overall management, who then injects it into every aspect of the business, or it can arise from the individual products, services, and operating groups of the company. In the first case a clear, crusading direction is set for the business to follow; in the latter case, the vision is a mission statement that summarizes what works about the existing business and how to make the most of it.

From a bottom-up viewpoint, Singapore-based Creative Technology was an early darling of the Asian technology marketing scene. The company pioneered the design, manufacture and marketing of PC audio cards that deliver stereo-quality sound, not just in Asia, but also worldwide. *Far Eastern Economic Review* ranked Creative Technology in 2001 as second in the Asia region as a firm whose management has long-term vision. When you look closely at the company, the vision does not focus on abstract plans to dominate the world, but rather very focused efforts to consistently offer the best sound cards at the best value for money. The company has diversified into other product areas, but the bulk of the revenue and the kudos for vision consistently come from the sound-card business. The vision of the company starts from the bottom up: if the product is right and the price is right, then the customers will consistently come.

KFC (which started as Kentucky Fried Chicken) also has a clear business focus: to dominate the quick service chicken restaurant business, but theirs starts from the top down. As a global brand, and part of Yum! Brands,Inc. (which includes Pizza Hut and Taco Bell), KFC is part of a corporation that has nearly 30,000 employees and operations around the world. Clearly, although founder Colonel Sanders has achieved almost mythical status, this is not a company comprised of people who come in every day to serve chicken and accidentally create a global brand. Everything from brand values, operational techniques, menus items and BIG M marketing strategies are cascaded from the corporate head office to franchisees and then to individual employees to customers. This BIG M Marketing vision works everywhere, but requires a few tweaks around the world.

In China, the company has placed a life-sized statue of founder Colonel Sanders outside almost every restaurant, but they certainly don't spend a lot of time or money trying to educate consumers about where the state of Kentucky is – this isn't part of their BIG M Marketing strategy. KFC is now the most popular international brand in China, according to ACNielsen Media International, and has more than 510 outlets in China as of October 2001 (compared with fewer than 400 McDonald's restaurants).

The American connection has proved useful in marketing terms, and KFC has imported the American tradition of Thanksgiving to China. This little m Marketing campaign has been so successful that customers now have to reserve a bucket of chicken in advance of Thanksgiving. The KFC brand has tapped the BIG M strategy of appealing to Chinese consumers' impressions of chicken as a dish that is usually more expensive than beef and only served on festive or special occasions.

Vision can work from the top down or from the bottom up. The essential factor is that the company and its executives have one, believe it, and pursue it single mindedly and relentlessly.

Tell a story you would like to hear

So much of the value of having a vision is about communicating it in a clear and compelling way. As a business leader, think carefully about what your vision is, what it means in down-to-earth terms that offer benefits to individuals, and then tell a story YOU would like to hear. Quantitative targets generally don't make compelling visions (unless it is along the lines of "Let's be the first company to sell 40 million mobile phone handsets in Malaysia"). Abstract business theories are equally irrelevant. Would you be motivated by the rallying cry. "To bring excellence and innovation and enhanced customer service to Asia's pulp and paper industry". If the story is interesting to you personally, it will help you to be passionate and credible about your business. And, if you tell an interesting story, analysts will take note, journalists will call for stories and quotes, and your employees will be able to explain where the company is going to customers, suppliers, and even their relatives who ask what they are doing.

Mao Chi-kuo, former Chairman of Chunghwa Telecom, is recognized in Taiwan as the man who "was trying to teach a dinosaur to dance." Chunghwa Telecom, Taiwan's formerly state-run telecom is renowned for lumbering along like an old dinosaur. Now that the island's telecom market has liberalized and Chunghwa Telecom has begun to privatize, the company finds itself losing ground to competitors in every aspect of its business. Mao realizes that Chunghwa Telecom must transform itself from a slow bureaucratic dinosaur into a modern corporation. Instead of merely dictating from above as a government minister might, Mao involved himself and the company's management personally in marketing campaigns and frequently communicated with Chunghwa's employees via e-mail. While not quite yet spinning pirouettes, the dinosaur's new corporate culture is making it increasingly nimble.

Clearly articulating the BIG M Marketing strategy also provides a guide for determining whether a little m Marketing tactic is appropriate. For example, if the vision is to build a profitable Mexican restaurant business in Thailand and budget is limited, running a week-long promotion in conjunction with the Mexican embassy that brings in new and interested customers is better than offering 50% off every item for a week. Since profit is the guiding vision, then discounting is not the road to go down.

Asian business is littered with companies that had grand visions and no reality – or conversely worked hard but for no higher purpose. Take the time to set a vision for your company, and your time will be rewarded tenfold by avoiding the inefficiencies of your executive team all heading in different directions. For further tips on integrating BIG M strategies with little m marketing tactics, see the Navigation Tools section at the end of this book.

MOVE UPSTREAM

"Politicians are the culprits and businessmen are the accomplices."
- Chung Ju Yung

"Grasshopper always wrong in argument with chicken."
- Book of Chan

The problem with the worst marketing plans in Asia is that they try to influence customer decisions that have already been made. If a consumer is trying to decide what car he/she likes and has been conditioned virtually since birth to believe that Mercedes-Benz is the preeminent car badge, then no amount of little m Marketing (price discounts, glossy brochures, witty ads or car-show appearances) is going to change that perception. The only way to change it is to move upstream in the way customer decisions are made, and in the supply chain, to influence factors that can force quantum shifts in the marketplace. BIG M Marketing often requires opening a new sales channel, influencing commercial legislation that may be limiting market share, or radically changing pricing structures (switching from low volume, high-margin pricing to low-margin, high-volume, for example).

Moving upstream requires an often-radical rethink of the market situation, and the formulation of a strategy that redefines the target customer, the competitive set, and/or the whole cost basis of the business to date. In the process, moving upstream re-invigorates the effectiveness of little m Marketing tactics, because new segments are opened up, rather than simply fighting for market share within the same segment.

The essence of moving your marketing upstream is to confirm the most important parameters of your BIG M success as early as possible in the marketing cycle, and validated by the most senior decision makers possible. Your goal is to lock in your company's market position and product relevance in a compelling way that competitors will have a hard way replicating. After markets mature and your company and products have been out in the marketplace for awhile, then the battleground will shift to little m Marketing and the use of tactics to grab market share from each other. When you move "upstream," however, you can help set the rules of the game, and meet customer needs in new and highly relevant ways that yield much greater incremental sales than simply slugging it out with other parity companies.

If you have a major marketing idea that will help transform the business, move upstream to the CEO, rather than trying to work your way upwards through a hierarchical organization from receptionist, to junior executive, to marketing manager. Work with the people who formulate and sign off on strategy, not just those who sign off on tactical plans and budgets. Write your company's marketing plan at the same time as the business plan, not as an administrative afterthought.

Here are some BIG M strategies for moving upstream.

Shock the price/value equation

Look for ways to "shock" the price/value equation, especially in mature markets in which prices have stabilized. If the whole market sector has been pushed toward the cheap/commodity marketplace end of the scale (consider the pre-Haagen-Dazs ice-cream market), then push your product to the other end and offer a significantly better product at a higher price. Of course you take a BIG M Marketing risk that consumers may not follow, but if you succeed, new levels of profit margin will be added, until competitors regroup and challenge your price point with a similar product at a lower price.

Sometimes moving upstream to re-define the marketplace for a particular good or service opens up new sales and profit opportunities that would be inaccessible if a company simply redoubled its little m Marketing efforts. A good example of a company using this strategy that is aggressively expanding into Asia is Starbucks. Suddenly a cup of coffee costs US$4, not US 80 cents. Sure, it may be somewhat better coffee, but part of the cost goes into shop design and construction, to ensure that the product also comes with a whole lifestyle experience. The rules of the game changed, and now the premium coffee shop category is a whole new sector, with companies such as Hong Kong's Pacific Coffee slugging it out with Starbucks on the same BIG M battlefield.

At the other end of the spectrum, a BIG M Marketing strategy can be to suddenly make a product that was previously out of the reach of your target consumer cheap and accessible. A good example of this is found in Japan's travel industry, where hundreds of thousands of "office ladies" (often single white-collar workers who don't have to bear the costs of running family households) travel regularly around the world to places their grandmothers only dreamed of going. The rise in tourism is due in part to rising incomes of single women with low expenses, but also due to cost-effective bulk packaging so that individuals can afford to travel in groups to places that would be unaffordable or inaccessible (language barriers) otherwise. The office lady on the group tour may be paying 25% less than the wealthy individual who plans and books the entire trip him or herself. The little m Marketing focus for these tour groups then becomes a mechanical task of making sure the target group is aware of their services and how to book, via advertising and direct marketing.

Discover new, less mature markets

An effective BIG M Marketing strategy for multinational companies in the region is to seek out new, less mature markets. In these new markets, consumers may have

- a pent-up demand for the product or service;
- new-found affluence that gives them spending power;
- a less sophisticated scope of product knowledge that allows inferior products to sell;
- less concern about consumer or health issues (e.g. tobacco companies entering the Third World) and;
- less disposable income and therefore willingness to buy "previous-generation" products.

From dogs as food to food for dogs

The bravest BIG M, little m Marketers are those who go where no marketer has gone before. Any practitioner can move into an established market and battle for market share, trying to steal customers from the other brand, and develop compelling marketing plans to keep the existing customer base intact. It's certainly not easy, but at least there is an established marketplace.

You are asking people who know they want to make a choice to select among brands. The hardest marketing challenge is to create a market, especially when culturally your target markets don't know they are targets, and probably initially don't want to be either. This is where you meet the boldest, savviest marketers.

Such are the people who market dog food in Korea. The recent World Cup brought onto the world stage the controversy about some Koreans' interest in eating dog meat, and also highlighted the growing pet ownership culture in Korea. Selling dog food to Koreans is not quite as extreme as the challenge of selling Scotch whisky to the Saudis, but it's close.

The tradition of keeping pets and feeding them special food is not innately part of the Korean culture, so before dog-food sales can truly take off, the marketplace needs to be educated on the benefits of domestic pet ownership. In Korea, many neighborhoods play host to stray dogs, which are given table scraps by residents, but the idea of keeping a dog in your own home as a pet has only started to gain acceptance in recent years.

The pet-food makers, such as Pedigree, have invested considerable sums into building a pet culture and educating pet owners about the importance of nutritious pet food. For example, they have provided dogs to schools and old-aged homes to demonstrate the benefit of having a group pet. They have underwritten psychological studies via universities to study the benefits of pet ownership in child development and family values. They have prepared reams of local language materials on the care and feeding of dogs, and on demonstrating the ease of taking care of a pet. They have also profiled local celebrities who have kept dogs to show the popularity of keeping pets. Many of these tactics seem basic and even humorous in the context of cultures that fully understand pet dog ownership, but in Korea much of this basic information and appreciation is not taken for granted, either by the target consumers or by the marketers.

Waking up to international eating habits

One way to move upstream is to help change the lifestyle habits of your target customers in ways that expand the overall market.

In the US and other global markets, the hallmarks of the cereal business are cutthroat competition for supermarket shelf space and aggressive price promotions to protect or build market share. Leading player Kellogg's has slimmed down its workforce in the US to keep costs low in order to allow maximum flexibility in pricing. The company has also added brand extensions such as Rice Krispy Treats that compete with other snack foods and build incremental revenue outside the cereal battlefield.

In Korea, Kellogg's has been working hard for many years to build its breakfast-cereal business. Here, and in other countries with evolving customer lifestyles and tastes, the BIG M marketing advantage for the cereal companies lies in helping lead dietary change, and moving the company upstream in the marketing process. Instead of fighting a price-driven war over single-digit changes in market share with other cereal companies, as they do in the US and elsewhere in the world, the players in Korea are contributing to building overall consumer demand and a new market. A traditional Korean breakfast most definitely does not include cereal, and although many Koreans are increasingly adding Western food to their diet, the majority still follows the same eating patterns as their parents.

Cereal brands such as Kellogg's got an early foothold in Korea, not as a breakfast favorite, but rather as an easy-to-eat afternoon or mid-morning snack. Younger people especially would take a few handfuls directly out of the box to stave off hunger between meals. In terms of both regularity of use and volume of consumption, this usage of the product does not have a lot of potential. Therefore the objective of much cereal marketing in Korea is to help educate consumers on the value of a balanced breakfast, Western style. If there is not time for a full Korean breakfast, cereal with milk provides a fast, nutritious meal. The BIG M Marketing strategy is to build awareness of the value of cereal (particularly Kellogg's) as a good way to start the day, with the focus on little m Marketing tactics that reach out to the main influencers on the choice of breakfast, including mothers, young people and nutrition educators.

Korea and New Zealand move upstream in Asia

The BIG M, little m Marketing strategy of moving upstream is not just limited to products, brands and companies. As countries and linked groups of economies such as ASEAN look for ways to move themselves up the value chain and get into higher value-added industries, government policy makers and politicians in Asia are looking for ways to move upstream.

Korea's rise over the last 20 years is a practical example of how entire economies can move up in the supply chain by force of will, planning and execution. Korea's economic growth in recent decades has been a sometimes tense interplay of government and corporate interests, and the reforms following the 1997 economic crisis have left the country with both vast domestic and international business potential but no immediately clear way forward. For much of its recent economic history, Korea has been a country in which little m Marketing took place in public and whatever the equivalent of marketing strategy was, it took place in smoke-filled back rooms as deals were made and markets carved up with little transparency or open competition.

Korea's economic growth undoubtedly owes the family-owned *chaebol* companies such as Samsung and Daewoo a debt of gratitude. In at least equal proportion in the formula for success were the Korean government's efforts to identify firms ripe for growth and then provide them with overt and covert assistance. This was Korea's equivalent of BIG M Marketing from the 1960s to the 1980s. The government was conscious that the country was in danger of being caught between the developed and developing countries. The government implemented policies that (according to one scholarly viewpoint) "cleared roadblocks to corporate growth and often provided monopolistic conditions (and resulting economies of scale) that were conducive to success."

With this powerful BIG M incentive to move upstream the *chaebol* companies grew quickly, further pushed along by hard work and engineering skill. In later years, the system has been wracked by dissent, with the *chaebol* reacting against their government sponsors in many cases, and many of the country's numerous SMEs that previously formed the backbone of the Korean economy feeling left behind in the new order. The threads of these disagreements are still factors in BIG M, little m Marketing in Korea today, compounded by debates over foreign ownership, openness of markets and increasing but not entirely open business transparency.

In this environment, marketing has grown up as a discipline with a firm emphasis on the little m Marketing tactics. Korean firms have focused on securing distribution and driving products and services through the supply chain. Traditionally, low cost goods drove Korean exports, although Samsung and a few other Korean companies are now among the best brand marketers in the world. International companies coming into Korea until very recently found marketing to be 70% public affairs, 20% labor relations and 10% of what is normally considered marketing, thanks to the onerous layers of government approvals and labor issues.

A company's fortunes in the business world were often inextricably tied up with how they were perceived by opinion leaders and decision makers in societal institutions outside the business world, such as government, media and academia. Even the structure of the marketing industry was different. In Korea, many of the strategic and creative BIG M Marketing functions that are usually handled by external agencies elsewhere in the world were tightly held by the in-house corporate advertising and marketing departments of Korean corporations. In this environment, BIG M Marketing was almost completely subsumed by the little m.

The insular, restricted marketplace that gave birth to Korean marketing is being transformed by reforms arising after the 1997 economic crisis, with growing globalization of Korean companies and the market opening to imported goods. In addition, the level of creativity in Korean marketing is beginning to rival the best in the world.

New Zealand is another economy that has transformed itself. In 1984, New Zealand was one of the most regulated economies in the world; today it is one of the most open. This is good news for BIG M, little m Marketers and bodes well for the future. A good example of New Zealand's practical approach was to make the painful decision of letting the country's protected car industry fall apart, rather than try to hold onto outdated protectionist measures. Instead, the resources that were propping up the automotive industry were re-deployed to refocus on high-tech manufacturing.

In worldwide terms, New Zealand is a relatively small market, but the government's free market principles and practical approach to opening the domestic market, matched with vigorously driving overseas promotion of exports, makes it one of the highest potential Asia BIG M little Marketing leaders.

A country's government can be an important contributor to the marketing of its economy, as well as the individual companies doing business there.

Lobby government change the marketing environment

Sometimes the environment is just too harsh for even the most enterprising marketing company to be successful. When the economic situation or local rules and regulations make it almost impossible to do business, one way of moving upstream is to turn to the government and lobby for more favorable conditions.

The large Korean manufacturers used this BIG M Marketing strategy in the early 1980s. Korea's automotive industry had been massively built up to service the needs of a growing export market for the low-cost, high-quality vehicles being produced. Car buyers in Asia's developing nations and in Latin America, as well as Europe and the US to a lesser degree, were snapping up Korean-made cars and trucks as cost-effective alternatives to the Japanese vehicles that started cheap, but had steadily progressed in price and quality leaving an opening in the low/moderate end of the market.

However, in the early 1980s, international demand began to plateau. The Korean automotive industry had been built almost entirely on a produce-and-sell model, rather than looking at what the market was demanding and then creating the right product in the right quantity to satisfy demand. When overseas orders slowed and cars began to pile up on the docks, the Korean automotive industry turned to the government for respite. It would have been virtually impossible for the Korean manufacturers to sell additional vehicles domestically, because Korean law required that car purchasers pay cash.This legislation historically made sense for several reasons. Emerging from the hardships of rebuilding after the Korean War, the government wished to limit ostentatious spending on unnecessary items, and to keep consumers' debt loads at a minimum. Public transportation was plentiful and adequate and the road system (prior to the massive upgrade initiated in conjunction with the staging of the 1988 Olympics) was not extensive enough to handle a large influx of vehicles. Because cars had to be purchased in cash in one lump payment, only corporations and the wealthiest individuals could afford them.

When the car industry needed to find a way to show continuous growth and to keep its assembly lines and autoworkers fully occupied, they appealed to the government to change the regulations to allow consumers to buy vehicles on an installment plan. Suddenly, a whole generation for whom owning a car was just a dream, found that their rising incomes and the ability to spread out the payments made it possible for them to buy cars; which they did quickly and in large numbers, choking the nation's highways. Whereas driving in 1988 was a swift process along wide, virtually empty roads prepared in time for the Olympics, soon the famous Seoul traffic jams mounted; but the industry achieved its marketing objectives by moving upstream of the problem.

Taxi, please

Another example in the automotive industry is Ford's efforts to get LPG Ford Falcons into service as taxi cabs in Hong Kong. Many years ago, the taxis in Hong Kong were made by Mercedes-Benz, known for their reliability and hard-wearing service. In recent years, however, the market has been virtually dominated by Toyota Crown taxis. They are relatively inexpensive when bought in large quantities, and spare parts are easy to get. Ford, which has only a tiny fraction of the Hong Kong vehicle market, successfully applied to get their vehicles approved for use as taxis and now examples can be seen regularly around the city, although the Toyotas still dominate. By doing so, Ford was able to "move upstream" to create a new market for its vehicles in a way that no amount of little m Marketing could have.

The key to getting the vehicles on the roads was aligning with the Hong Kong government's push to get more environmentally friendly taxis and minibuses, powered by LPG. Taxis with properly installed and maintained LPG equipment produce on the order of 15% less CO_2 than unleaded petrol. Hong Kong is allocating US$93 million to the SAR's 18,000 taxi owners to convert the entire taxi fleet from diesel to LPG power by 2005 to reduce greenhouse gas output. Each dedicated LPG-fueled version of the Ford Falcon can reduce global warming potential by up to 20%, as compared with conventional diesel taxis.

The first 20 LPG Ford Falcon taxis were introduced into Hong Kong in March 2000, as a result of cooperation between Ford, Hong Kong car dealership Wallace Harper, the Australian Trade Commission and the Hong Kong Government. Responding to the government's call for LPG-powered vehicles and acting decisively on the announcement of government subsidies provided to taxi owners to purchase new vehicles gave Ford a BIG M competitive advantage.

Move up the supply chain

Another BIG M move upstream strategy is to focus on moving up the supply chain. Let's look at the footwear industry's manufacturing supply chain as an example.

Illustration 6

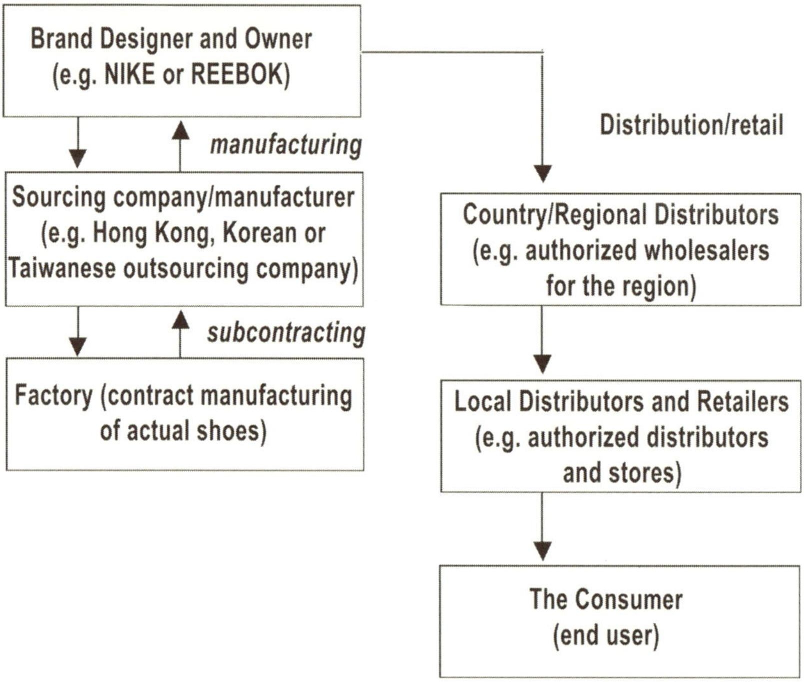

The brand owner and designer (such as Nike or Reebok) creates a product line and determines the manufacturing specifications (materials, colors, assembly guidelines) and also creates the BIG M Marketing strategy for the product and a core group of little m Marketing tactics (such as advertising visuals, point-of-sale materials, ideas for launch events, and promotions).

The specifications for the product are passed to manufacturers, who bid for the contract to make the shoes. They in turn subcontract various aspects of the process to other companies (such as leather work, plastic molding, trim and assembly) that either have specialized expertise, or which can do the work more cost effectively than the main contracted manufacturer.

Many of the footwear manufacturers themselves moved upstream as the labor costs in their countries increased to the point where they could no longer cost effectively manufacture on behalf of the international brands. Instead, they had to decide which of three courses of action to follow:

- Drop or lose the contracts for international brands.
- Start making their own brand name items (with less brand recognition but more profit margin per unit for them since they eliminate one layer of the supply chain).
- Change roles and manage the manufacturing process on behalf of the brands, but by subcontracting to other less expensive suppliers in Vietnam and Indonesia.

Although some footwear companies chose to go "upstream" on the brand side and start their own consumer product lines for domestic sale or export, most chose to use their array of contacts, suppliers, and specialized knowledge to manage the manufacturing process. It should be added that many US companies manufacture in multiple locations so that when their quota of imports from any one country for that category of goods is exhausted, the supply is not interrupted. This briefly gives the middlemen in the supply chain a renewed role, but one that will likely diminish again as manufacturers increasingly locate their production in quota-free China as the WTO provisions roll out.

Some Taiwanese companies have pursued the BIG M "going up the supply chain" strategy all the way to brand level. Taiwan built large OEM businesses manufacturing tennis rackets, golf clubs, fishing rods and mountain bikes that were then sold under other companies' brand names. Today, some Taiwan-originated brands are recognized worldwide, such as Giant for bicycles and Kennex for tennis racquets.

Sometimes no amount of little m Marketing will help you increase your market share or revenue beyond a certain level. Moving upstream with new distribution strategies is a fundamental BIG M Marketing move that can open up whole new market sectors with far greater potential than trying to achieve incremental growth with your existing target customers.

Refocus when your customer refocuses

The moving upstream BIG M Marketing principle has been successfully demonstrated by Global Sources (previously known as Asian Sources), a Hong Kong-based company that has proactively reinvented its business proposition in order to stay relevant to its core customers.

The company started in 1971 as a publisher of a print magazine carrying advertising from Asian manufacturers and distributed to volume importers around the world. As a conduit for information about Asian products and suppliers, the company grew as part of – and in many ways as a catalyst for – the export-led development of the Asian tiger economies (Hong Kong, Korea, Singapore, and Taiwan) in the following three decades. Over this time the company grew and segmented its market, publishing magazines for specific "vertical" sectors ranging from electronic components to housewares to telecom products.

As the company developed, Asian Sources attracted fierce competitors ranging from local "me-toos," competing on price, to publishing operations run by government-mandated trade promotion organisations. Over the course of many years, the company became adept at little m Marketing techniques, channeled via a sales force of nearly 600 sales representatives in Taiwan, China, Hong Kong, Korea, Japan, and Southeast Asia.

Everything changed for the company then known as Global Sources in 1995 when the Internet began to emerge as an information tool for business. More specifically, the Internet, comprising both e-mail for cheap and instant communications and the World Wide Web for its product-cataloging capabilities, meets many of the needs of global traders as if it had been invented specifically for this purpose. Asian Sources saw more clearly than most that this new medium could transform the whole business of trade, and would at the very least change the trade magazine business forever.

The company's primary BIG M Marketing insight was its realization that despite the fact that the vast majority of its (substantial) revenues came from publishing, it was not a magazine company as such. Since 1971, the company's core competence had been linking buyers and suppliers together globally. It had been successful in this mission only to the extent that it had enabled buyers to identify products and suppliers that could meet consumer demand in western retail markets. The emergence of the Internet offered a way to do this more efficiently and effectively than ever before.

Inspired by this BIG M vision, in 1995 the company transformed its operations. In doing so it risked up to US$100 million per year in print-driven revenues. It risked losing market position not only to the print competitors who continued to snap at its heels, but also a new breed of venture-capital-funded Internet-based competitors. It also jeopardized the powerful brand it had built over three decades among the import-export community when Asian Sources changed its name to Global Sources in 1999.

Today, the majority of Global Sources' revenues come from the Internet. Global Sources still publishes magazines and CD-ROMs that are positioned to support the core Web offering. But not only is the company supporting more buying-and-selling relationships than ever before, it is also now expanding to provide a wider range of electronically-enabled trade transaction services that promise a new base of revenue and profit growth.

The fact that Global Sources is around and thriving is the result of that move upstream to a business vision of the true value a company can bring to its customers and its willingness to "bet the ranch" on that value. Global Sources' experience shows that unlike little m Marketing, BIG M Marketing is fundamentally about business strategy, and is not confined just to the marketing department. At Global Sources it pervades and is implemented by the entire company in the quest to match buyers and sellers by whatever means possible and profitable.

The process of moving upstream should be continuous. Sometimes management may decide that little m Marketing can still be used to drive further sales or expand market share, but other times a more radical approach is needed. A solid philosophy of "If it's not broken, then still fix it" is prudent to make sure your company is not left behind by market changes or misses competitive advantages.

GO, GO, GO!

"Our greatest glory is not in never falling, but in rising every time we fall."

- Confucius

"Fall seven times, stand up the eighth time."

- Japanese proverb

Throughout this book, "Mm Winners" are held up as the heroes of marketing in Asia, and much emphasis is placed on the importance of having the right BIG M Marketing strategy. However, nothing can diminish the value of *doing*. "Doers" can survive where "Dreamers" fail. All the strategy in the world is worth nothing without sustained, consistent execution. It's about getting the balance right. Especially in Asia's high velocity, price-based marketplaces, the law of averages sometimes rules over pre-meditated strategy. Make as many chances for your product or services as possible, and then follow every opportunity aggressively through to its conclusion, either successful or not. Do enough, fast enough and your business will be propelled forward, and if your strategy is wrong you will at least find out the result more quickly and can head off in a more profitable direction. Factors such as luck, hard work and favorable market timing reward those marketers with a predilection to action. Put another way: "Go, go, go!"

Don't just sip it!

A perhaps apocryphal story about an executive at one of France's major Cognac houses illustrates the importance of not overthinking strategy in less mature markets. A descendent of the founders and member of a venerable family, the executive was in the Cognac region, accompanied by a delegation of Taiwanese journalists and trade guests who had come from Taipei to tour the region and learn more about the product's origins. Taiwan is a major market for Cognac, and it was important for both trade relations and product promotion objectives that these visitors leave with a good impression from their trip. In Taiwan, Cognac is central to some business entertaining, both in that it shows the taste and generosity of the host and can be the focus of a relaxed, relationship building night on the town. Of course, the cost of the company of a beautiful woman is often built into the extortionate price of a bottle of premium XO Cognac in a nightclub, but that is an aspect of BIG M, little m Marketing outside the scope of this book. Cognac is also frequently drunk at dinner in large quantities with ice and water, like wine or beer.

The group visiting Cognac went to a bar/restaurant one evening and enjoyed large amounts of brandy, served the Taiwanese way. As the evening wore on the Taiwanese guests looked into a corner and saw a French man and a woman very obviously romantically involved. They had the traditional balloon glasses filled with just a small amount of brandy, and they rolled the glasses around, using the heat of their hands to release the aroma, staring into each other's eyes. They took very small sips and talked more than they drank as they enjoyed their nightcap. One of the journalists looked up from his water glass full of Cognac and ice and asked, "What are those two people doing?" To which the Cognac executive replied, "Pay no attention to them," and quickly sought to distract them from learning new habits that could reduce their consumption. "Can I get you another drink?"

"Shenme Dou You!"- eBay Taiwan "Has It All"

eBay's launch in Taiwan is a good example of what can be done when a simple strategy is aggressively and thoroughly executed. In April 2002, eBay entered the Taiwan market with the purchase of NeoCom Technology, operator of Taiwan's leading auction site, uBid. Soon thereafter, eBay made the decision to switch uBid's community of users to the eBay trading software platform and rebrand the site as eBay Taiwan. Simultaneously, the competitive pressure was heating up with rival Yahoo-Kimo declaring to the media just weeks before eBay's launch that it aimed to go head-to-head with them in Taiwan's online auction space.

With launch time looming, there was an urgent need to develop creative marketing promotions and PR opportunities that would significantly raise eBay's brand profile and help educate existing and potential users about the value and functionality of its online auction site. eBay's community of users needed to find lots of exciting, desirable and exclusive things for sale when they visited the site. All promotional activities were grouped under the tagline "eBay Shenme Dou You," or "eBay has it all," which reflects the abundance of items available on the site.

The criteria for promotions were that they should drive traffic in eBay's key categories; help eBay retain current users; bring new users to the eBay community; and generate publicity. The approach was to form a SWAT team that would "go, go, go!" to reach out to as many relevant local and multinational potential marketing partners as possible. The team brainstormed a core group of promotional ideas that were further developed, and then pitched again and again to dozens of target companies and organizations. The pitching task also often included introducing the eBay brand's business model as the company was not well known in Taiwan prior to the launch.

By launch time, the pitching process had yielded a blitz of promotions over a four-week period, including a new model of IBM ThinkPad notebook computers and an as-yet-unreleased Sony digital camcorder model. Both items were unavailable for purchase anywhere except the eBay site in Taiwan at the time. Other hot items included 100th anniversary collectible teddy bears auctioned for charity with certificates of authenticity signed by a popular Taiwan TV host; a chance to meet and greet with Hollywood film director John Woo, movie paraphernalia from Warner Bros and 20th Century Fox; exclusive movie premiere tickets; and celebrity-signed music promotional items and CDs. The unique, newsworthy promotions earned widespread media publicity and helped build the eBay brand and website traffic during a critical period.

Absolutely fab, but out of luck

Semiconductor chip manufacturers must make very large bets on their BIG M strategies, and then "go, go, go!" The chip fabricators in Taiwan and Korea require billions of dollars to erect the latest generation "fabs." Although there is some flexibility in the range of products made, they are generally locked into the terrifying economics of large investments that must be continuously generating a return based on high volumes in an industry where the trends shift with every breath of wind. RDRAM (Rambus Dynamic Random Access Memory) chips are a good example. Taiwanese semiconductor foundries such as TSMC and UMC incorporated the promising technology from Rambus. After ramping up production to supply the industry and to build up volumes to the level where prices could be dropped and profit margins increased, demand did not rise as fast as expected from PC and server manufacturers as their customers in turn weighed up the cost/benefits of slightly better memory but at significantly higher cost, and decided the difference was not enough to make a wholesale change to the new technology.

The situation was complicated by lawsuits, arguments over the technology, and recalls. Intel Pentium 4 chips were originally designed to function only with RDRAM, but now contain SDRAM, the most common form of memory on the market today. Computers with these chips cost less and have caused Intel executives to blame some of their company's recent problems on adapting to Rambus. The chip manufacturers had carefully done their BIG M Marketing homework by assessing anticipated demand, and then working closely with the chip makers, equipment manufacturers and software makers to optimize the benefits of RDRAM to the end customer and promote the new technology throughout every phase of the marketing cycle. However, the global slowdown in new PC orders accompanied by the slower-than-expected take-up of RDRAM turned their luck against them.

When bad luck happens to good companies

There are times when no amount of proactive effort or wishful thinking can change the overall marketing environment. Sometimes good companies make all the right management moves, but are trapped in the wrong marketing environment. Astra International, the Indonesian auto manufacturer, is a good example of a company doing everything possible to change its luck and get back on its feet in a tough economic environment.

Following the 1997 Asia financial crisis, Astra restructured with the help of international bankers, cutting its debt by 20% (to US$900 million), and attracting foreign investment. In the early stages, revenues increased by 91% and year 2000 car sales went up by 169%.

However, this progress is now being challenged by:

- slowing car sales
- political uncertainty
- economic stagnation

- fluctuations in the Rupiah
- weakening investor confidence

With odds like that stacked against a business, no amount of BIG M or little m Marketing is going to change the company's luck.

Making your own luck

As marketing becomes increasingly focused on measurement, control, return on investment, and bottom line results, luck has been relegated to a far corner. In reality, luck is one of the most likely ways of achieving BIG M, little m success. Of course, as most lucky people know, you create your own luck and the best campaigns come out of doggedly trying various strategies and countless tactics before the right mix is discovered.

In Chinese and other business cultures in Asia, many people have a fervent belief that they can create their own luck, or at least mitigate the forces that might cause them to fail. For example, a glance around a Chinese office can reveal the touch of the *Feng Shui* master, from the coins taped over the doorway for luck, to the unexpectedly placed blue rectangle of carpet or statue of a horse.

Marketers also look to give themselves some luck and make their customers feel lucky by offering their products with price tags that end in lucky numbers. In the West, consumers are all too familiar with prices that end in "99". Called the "underestimation effect," the idea is that consumers will psychologically accept the idea of the base dollar amount being the price, and not take the 99 cents of the next unit of the price listed into account. Whatever. In a recent comparison survey of US and Asian price digit endings (yes, there is such a thing…the curious can see the bibliography for details), US prices ended in "0" 42% of the time, the largest score. At 37.4% the digit "9" came in second, and all other numbers were far behind.

In Asia the results were very different, both from the US model and from country to country. In Hong Kong, 3% of retail prices in the study ended in "0", and 14.8% ended in "8". In Cantonese Chinese, the number eight (*ba*) is a homonym for "to multiply" and thus very lucky. Prior to the

1970s all prices were set by the government, based on cost, so the final digits were more or less random. Now that merchants have the option, they vastly prefer choosing a lucky final digit over the ending "9" whatever the psychologists say about the "underestimation effect." Luck must also be an important component of profit, because by pricing goods ending in "8" retailers are losing a potential 1% on every sale compared to the US.

The trend is visible across Asia. In all countries surveyed (China, Hong Kong, Japan, Malaysia, and Singapore) "8" endings exceeded the proportion of "9" endings, except Singapore, and even there the "8" ending was twice as common as it is in America. Cantonese is used in southern China, and to some extent in the other countries, except Japan, which helps explain the prevalence of "hope for luck" pricing. In Japan, "8" is also a prevalent price ending (24.4% of prices in the survey ended in "8" as opposed to 1.8% ending in "0"): the Japanese *kanji* character for "8" resembles a mountain and symbolizes growth and prosperity.

In another study among Chinese consumers, A and S were found to be considered lucky letters, and F and Z unlucky. Lucky alphanumeric products names were perceived to have better quality and chance of success than non-lucky names.

Marketers all over the world need all the luck they can get and in Asia brand names and price endings should not be ignored for their cultural significance and appeal. However, really making your own luck is based on gaining clear market insight and using your company's scarce resources cleverly so you can end up in the right market position at the right time. Here are some BIG M strategies for making your own luck.

Play the field, but don't bet the farm

In the same way that the roulette gambler places his bets on all reds or even numbers, marketers can put in place low cost pilot programs across many options of changing tastes and market conditions. Once you spot a trend gaining momentum, shift resources and crank up the little m tactics. Advantage: you won't get caught at a dead standstill by emerging trends. Disadvantage: it can be distracting and inefficient to "hedge your bets" with multiple programs rather than go into depth and quality with one approach.

Act like the secret police

Follow the lead of the marketers in the most perilous and changeable markets, such as youth marketing and financial-services marketing. Youth marketers such as sneaker makers and record labels practically live with their customers, continually doing research, holding focus groups and hiring "incognito" trend watchers to go out and observe their potential customers as they make every decision in their daily lives. They are looking for lifestyle cues and influences that will affect customer demand for their products within days. Sometimes major trends will be signaled by subtle shifts. As the Chinese proverb says, the trick is "knowing that Autumn is coming just from a falling leaf."

Prime the pump

Before you can make your own luck, you have to get potential customers interested and involved. Here little m Marketing tactics are the heroes. Offer a substantial discount as part of a trial offer. Bundle your new product or service with others that already have a customer base.

The Post-it was an example of a product success waiting to happen when the right BIG M strategy and marketing push was applied to it. A 3M researcher developed a "low-tack" re-usable adhesive that was strong enough to hold papers together but not so strong that it tore the papers when they were pulled apart. The original idea was to market the adhesive as a tackless bulletin board or spray-on solution. A couple of years after the substance was discovered, a 3M researcher named Arthur Fry was in church, fumbling with the bookmarks he had placed in his hymnal to mark the music for that Sunday. He needed bookmarks that would stick, but not damage the book. Mr. Fry tried the "low-tack" adhesive with a small piece of paper, and the Post-it note was born. The product hit the market in the late 1970s but did not catch on in its first few years of distribution. Then 3M "primed the pump" by barraging offices and homes with samples. Once people tried them and appreciated their usefulness, sales took off.

Give the people what they want before they know it

Marketing in this book is defined as: "Identifying and anticipating customer needs and meeting them, profitably." The "making your own luck" strategy is all about the *anticipating* part of the equation.

For example, before the Sony Walkman was invented no consumer ever said they needed a small, portable private music system. The headphones were originally conceived by Sony engineers to get around the problem of the poor sound quality of the miniature speakers they were trying to incorporate into a miniature stereo system. Once the product was created, Sony went out to test whether or not the product actually met a consumer need in the marketplace. This is called an unsought product. Many millions of Walkman units later, it's clear the demand was there.

Tell them they probably can't have it

The idea of creating special limited editions to drive sales is nothing new, but it can be an effective way to create your own luck. The limited supply creates an added perceived value and adds an urgency to the purchase decision. In Asia, an extreme and effective example of this is the Good Enough label. In Osaka, the label's designer Hiroshi decided to open a store that is only open Wednesday through Saturday. On Wednesdays that week's product is displayed – often a new T-shirt design – and it inevitably sells out by the end of the day. The little m tactic is simply to create scarcity, and it generates lines of customers around the door on Wednesday before the shop opens.

Similarly, in Japan, notebook-computer manufacturers will create special models in limited editions of 25,000 or so, and can do so knowing they will all sell out whereas the usual rule of thumb for the industry is that you need to sell around 10 times that number to be profitable. Part of it is the computer industry responding to Japan's "supercycle" product lifecycle, but part of it is the manufacturers making their own luck.

Most management textbooks and "how-to" books from industry gurus would have you believe that successful marketing can be engineered to within an inch of success, based on research, best practice and hard work. The gambling aspect of marketing can be unscientific at best. The reality is that a stroke of luck can often be the decisive factor in business success, and a shifting of the wind in the wrong direction can wipe out millions of dollars. Every day as business people, we make small and large bets that can have far-reaching repercussions depending on their outcome. The results can be staggeringly positive, or crushingly negative.

If you "go, go, go!" are you guaranteed to get lucky? No, but the fast and flexible BIG M, little m Marketing company will push relentlessly ahead and constantly be looking for opportunity in adversity and ways to harness the strengths it has to catch wave of the prevailing market trends.

IT'S THE CUSTOMER, STUPID

"The reputation of a thousand years may be determined by the conduct of one hour."

- Japanese proverb

Imagine shooting a gun at a target from 100 yards away. Then imagine you are riding a wild horse while doing so. And the target is mounted on the side of a moving truck. And the target is only four inches across. And it's nighttime. That's about the scope of the challenge of reaching and servicing customers in Asia today. Just about every variable of customer relationship management (both in the consumer and B2B sectors) is shifting all at the same time:

- The consumer profile is changing and broadening as per capita incomes rise across the region.
- Although the Japanese have lead the way on consumer issues, elsewhere in the region, the nascent consumer movement has only recently stepped up the pace for enhanced quality, service and warranties.
- Companies are under pressure to demonstrate care about the community and for the environment, adding a new layer of cost largely unfamiliar to Asia businesses.
- The business customer is still likely to be SME, but also includes US and European multinationals expanding into the region, and Asia-based conglomerates.
- Customer service is increasingly important, but price is still a major determinant for purchasing decisions.
- Global best practice in customer service is making inroads into the region, but Asia-based innovations in this area are at a very early stage.
- Domestic competition is being intensified and compounded by international competitors.

- Technology is providing new tools for customer service (such as Web-based eCRM) but it is not yet clear what the winning technologies and what the return on investment in these new systems will be.

In this fluid and dynamic marketing environment, knowing and satisfying the customer's needs are critical. The BIG M, little m Marketer may be making every effort to put in place long-term, effective strategies, supported by the hard-hitting tactics that yield immediate business results. However, even if the strategy and tactics are perfectly aligned, if the customer has moved or is missed, then all is lost. So how can you gear up your enterprise to keep your customers satisfied while at the same time striving for true BIG M, little m Marketing?

Talk to me

Communications are an essential part of the marketing mix. In Asia through much of the twentieth century there has been a widening chasm between the intimate, personal service provided by the local neighborhood merchant and the clumsy, authoritative marketing of the large corporation. In the B2B sector it is common for marketing as we know it to become almost completely subsumed by the personal relationships between business managers. Companies are now increasingly realizing that they must talk in clear and meaningful ways to the individual consumer.

As far back as 1970 Alvin Toffler in his book *Future Shock* coined the phrase "demassification," referring to the fact that the mass production, mass marketing, and mass communications that had been the hallmarks of the post-World War II era were becoming less relevant. It was time to look at how to reach smaller, more targeted groups and individuals. Consumers were becoming immune to marketing tools such as broadcast TV advertising and mega-brands that promised to be all things to all people. It's increasingly clear that no one's behavior will ever be changed by simply submitting them to a string of broadcast messages and as the authors of the book and website *The Clue Train Manifesto* (www.cluetrain.com) argue, companies need to have an interactive conversation in order to be persuasive.

Dell Computer's custom delivery of PCs assembled according to each individual's order illustrates how "mass customization" and having a "conversation with customers" can be effectively rolled out in Asia. Amazon.com, with its personalized features that "learn" about the past behaviors of regular customers is another example, although the lack of local warehouses and logistics makes ordering some items from the US impractical.

In Asia, one company that has effectively engaged carefully targeted consumers in a "conversation" is ebabyasia. The company started as a "bricks-and-mortar" Hong Kong-based retailer of specialty baby products that meet world-class safety standards. It later expanded to Taiwan and Singapore, and built a comprehensive website that serves as an additional sales channel and also as a medium for consumers to understand the value of safe children's products.

Many of the baby products made and sold in Asia do not adhere to international safety standards, and discerning parents will seek out the safest and best products if they know where to find them. ebabyasia's BIG M Marketing strategy is to offer products that by-and-large retail at higher prices than average, yet deliver on the promise of safety that is worth the premium to most parents.

Early on ebabyasia learned the importance of having a clear, direct line of communication open to their customers and prospects. ebabyasia is a specialized business, and the customer has very specialized needs; the perfect match for a "conversational" marketing relationship. ebabyasia's little m Marketing has been focused on precisely reaching potential customers – couples expecting children, pregnant women, and new parents – at exactly the moment they are interested in safe baby products. The company experimented with mass advertising, but discovered that this approach resulted in a lot of wastage, and a diluted message. What works best is highly targeted and specific communications. Leaflets in antenatal classes, hospital maternity wards, and doctors' offices. Ads in baby magazines. Ads in family-oriented home-delivered circulars. Every piece of communication prominently features the website address, and consumers can go there to order or to learn more about a product's features and safety benefits.

A BIG M Marketing advantage of this approach has been that ebabyasia is generally able to put its stores at relatively lower-cost locations.

Since they know where to find their customers and how to talk to them, there is little need for expensive ground-floor real estate to capture random walk-by trade. The website provides a highly specific destination of interest to the well-defined target audience. ebabyasia has learned through systematic analysis of their sales trends and continuous interactive experience with customers in their retail locations to understand what their customers care about and are motivated to buy.

Pull, don't push

Many Asia-Pacific marketers have been blind to the importance of having conversations with customers due to the rigidity of the product distribution model in Asia. Major retailers and trading companies served as the "gatekeepers" to sales channels, and the reasons for allocating shelf space or featuring one product over another was often based on the relationship with the supplier rather than the relationship with the end customer. With a limited range of choice, customers generally picked the options offered from them since they didn't have the "clean slate" option to talk with wholesalers and retailers about their preferences and how they can be met.

As the competitive frame loosens up, understanding customers and meeting their needs will increasingly become a BIG M Marketing point of competitive advantage. The old-fashioned mass production and mass marketing mantra will continuously shift toward a customer-focused approach that pulls through the supply chain those goods and services that customers want.

A useful exercise is to put yourself in the customer's shoes and ask the following questions:

- How will this product or service change my life?
- How much do you expect me to pay for the product's benefits?
- How is this different from every other product?
  - More/fewer benefits?
  - Higher/lower price?

- Do I need it? Do I want it?
- Is it easy to buy and get customer service?

Now, compare the answers to your BIG M Marketing goals. If the customer's answers and the marketing department's answers are different, it's time for a BIG M makeover.

The essence of this worldwide customer-led revolution has been captured well in Patricia Seybold's book *Customers.com* with this checklist of must-dos:

- Target the right customer
- Own the total customer experience
- Streamline the business processes that affect the consumer
- Let the customers help themselves
- Help the customer do his job
- Deliver personalized service
- Foster community

In Asia, this customer-led revolution is in its early stages. Some formal, organized consumer rights movements and issues-oriented campaigns have been around since the 1970s, but with a few exceptions they have not gained much attention or momentum. Recent examples such as protests over genetically modified food are a different kind of activism than consumer demands and complaints about pricing policies and customer service. Asia is by and large much less litigious than the US and it is to be expected that fewer consumer-related lawsuits occur in the region given the relatively early stage of development of the customer rights movement.

In Asia, the consumer's point of view is represented more by actual purchasing patterns than by non-government organisations, or consumer pressure groups articulating their points of view. For example, in

Indonesia, consumers do have real purchasing power, but because of the low median income, many are not able to lay out the lump of cash required to purchase a large supply of a particular item. They want to buy laundry powder, shampoo and cigarettes, but many cannot afford to buy a bulk pack. Therefore, a local roadside industry of individuals who buy cigarettes by the pack and then re-sell them one stick at a time has sprung up. Trial-size bottles and sachets of international FMCG company products are also frequently brought in as parallel imports to the official distribution system, and resold as single-use portions.

Across the region, marketers are increasingly listening to consumers and changing their practices and prices to meet consumer needs. And, increasingly savvy marketers are coming to realize that although the upper middle-class urban consumer in Tokyo, Singapore or Sydney may have considerable spending power and behave similarly to one another, there is a less obvious segment that in the aggregate offers huge marketing potential. This exciting marketing segment is the far-flung, less affluent rural consumers around the region. An example of a company reaching out to this market segment is Unilever Indonesia, which has now developed lower-cost products, smaller-sized packages, and cost-efficient distribution to reach the 128 million rural dwelling consumers. In India, Hindustan Lever sends every management trainee out for six to eight weeks to a rural, low-income Indian village, to truly understand the way people live and what they want. In the Philippines, Lever distributes sachets of Surf laundry detergent in rice sacks via a network of specially built heavy-duty bicycles that can cost effectively reach remote areas. Amway is taking a similar approach in India, selling sachet-sized containers of its products through an efficient regionwide "relationship-selling" network of independent distributors.

These examples all represent BIG M Marketing milestones for companies beginning to listen to their customers, and finding ways to have their products *pulled* through the distribution chain by demand from consumers who really want them, at prices they can afford. This change in mindset is a good starting point, but it's just the beginning of the coming revolution that will unfold over the next five to ten years for most companies in just about every industry sector.

Listen, don't lecture

Listening is becoming increasingly a part of B2B and services marketing. Upstream Asia recently had an instructive experience when we handled the launch marketing for a new e-business strategy service targeting SMEs. Grant Thornton, a leading international accounting consultancy specializing in SMEs, commissioned Upstream Asia to come up with a cost-efficient campaign to launch and promote the company's new "e*tech" services.

Grant Thornton had already launched e*tech services in the US and the UK to help companies make or take maximum advantage of the power of the Internet to make their businesses efficient. The swift growth of the Internet in the 1990s across all business sectors meant that even the smallest company could expand its use of the Internet beyond e-mail to manage inventory, customer relations and, ultimately, online commerce. However, by early 2001 when Grant Thornton was ready to bring the e*tech practice to Hong Kong, clouds were gathering over the dotcom dream. Stock valuations technology and Internet companies had taken a battering and businesses were taking a more critical look at their technology-related investments. This situation created significant challenges for Grant Thornton:

- Clients' perception of the added value of e*tech services was under the microscope, given the uncertainty in the Internet sector.
- As a midsize international financial adviser, Grant Thornton had a lower level of awareness in the business community compared to the "Big Five" firms.
- Although the e*tech practice was already proven in the US and UK, there were no existing clients or case studies to demonstrate local success at the time of the launch.

The decision was taken to undertake a research-based marketing project that would precisely illuminate and clarify the issues facing the SME target audience. This approach was designed to help illustrate and dramatize the need for Grant Thornton's service and define the company as an industry leader. One issue the research identified came across particularly clearly:

potential clients were confusing a loss of confidence in the stock market with the true benefits that clear e-business strategies would bring to companies.

Still, respondents across all industries overwhelmingly agreed that "having an e-business strategy is essential to long-term financial and commercial success," despite whatever short-term setbacks the technology and Internet sectors may have experienced. All of the managers with companies currently active in e-business, and 89% of companies *not* yet active in e-business, either agreed or strongly agreed with this statement.

The report results encouraged Grant Thornton executives to press ahead with e*tech services, because the findings showed that their target audience was not about to give up on formulating e-business strategies just because of the dotcom downturn. A little bit of listening went a long way, and the research also focused the BIG M Marketing strategy. The challenge was not to convince clients that they needed to go ahead with e-business strategies, but rather to raise specific, targeted awareness of e*tech services as the solution to the SME's challenge.

Build communities of like-minded customers and prospects

Another BIG M Marketing approach to reaching the target customer by starting an interactive conversation is for companies to encourage and accelerate the same process that happens naturally among groups of consumers: the sharing of information and experience and the forming of communities. As consumers tire of the "one-to-many" broadcast advertising approaches of the past, the connectivity of the Internet is stepping in as a powerful tool for "many-to-many" communications and companies can provide the platform for communities to form and grow. Ultimately, this is a much softer and less sales-oriented approach to marketing, but it is what increasingly sophisticated consumers in the region demand.

Mercedes-Benz in Taiwan has successfully pursued this strategy. One of the world's most prestigious brands, Mercedes-Benz realized the value of building a direct communication forum for customers. Mercedes-Benz Taiwan launched its first online marketing campaign via Microsoft MSN's portal (www.msn.com.tw) to increase membership of the previously offline-only Mercedes-Benz Motorsports Club and to reinforce the brand's premium/

performance positioning with information about the company's Formula One racing team.

The little m Marketing tactics included links on the MSN homepage, chat and community newsletters, a special Mercedes-Benz microsite inside MSN and streaming videoclips of the Mercedes-Benz team in action. By going online and providing an interactive forum for people interested in Mercedes-Benz, the number of club members more than doubled, and page views of the Mercedes-Benz materials approached half a million a month. The tactics drove visitors to the website, but the real benefit of this community activity was to increase potential customers' brand affinity and loyalty, further strengthening the cornerstone of the Mercedes-Benz's success.

Customers don't care what the origin of enhanced goods or services is, whether it's from better technology, human contact, or lower prices. Identifying BIG M Marketing trends such as fragmentation of markets, deregulation and mass customization is certainly not the customer's job. Customers may continuously send you clues about the trends, but they may be the last to spot the patterns, and no amount of market research will wrap up the strategy with a big bow for you. Ultimately, the BIG M Marketing responsibility for spotting the way to achieve competitive advantage lies with the marketer.

STEAL THE WHEEL!

"The onlookers see the chess game more clearly than the players themselves."

- Chinese proverb

"There is nothing new under the sun."

- The Bible, Ecclesiastes 1

One of the most useful Asia rules of BIG M, little m Marketing is "Steal the Wheel!" Do not feel for a moment that you have to reinvent the wheel, and besides, that is a tremendously inefficient way to do business. Chances are that just about any strategic or tactical challenge you are facing has been faced and solved hundreds of times before. Many countries in Asia have a long and not particularly proud heritage as counterfeiters and pirates of the intellectual property rights of other companies. That is not what "Steal the Wheel" is all about. It's about learning from the lessons of others and getting inspiration from the "Mm Winners." If you feel guilty about stealing the wheel, think of it in terms of adopting "regional or global best practice." It's the same concept with a fancier title, and the foundation of most MBA courses.

However, the Asian marketer must also beware of borrowing ideas, because every concept has to be filtered through sieves of culture, market situation and local relevance. This is particularly true in the case of Western marketing best practice, which cannot always be transplanted and expected to succeed.

Not everything you do has to be startlingly original or wildly creative. Your bosses and your shareholders will judge you ultimately on the bottom line business effectiveness, not on whether you deserve a Pulitzer Prize for originality.

In the early days of television, a man once offered a prize for anyone who could come up with a plot idea that had not already been thought of by Shakespeare. He was looking for something really new for his shows, but was convinced that there were no truly new ideas. The prize was never collected, as entrant after entrant was shown how their "original" idea had actually appeared in *Hamlet*, or *A Midsummer Night's Dream*.

The same is true of strategies and tactics: everything that is old becomes new, as a few basic concepts are adapted again and again for new generations and new applications. For example, online marketplace eBay is in many ways the epitome of the best way to harness the commercial power of the Internet. But strip away the technology and the auction method of purchasing goods and services is one of the world's oldest and most efficient.

The outside "skin" of your marketing campaign should be distinctive and fresh, but built on a solid base of proven approaches to similar problems. Spend your time making your BIG M, little m Marketing strategies and tactics run together seamlessly and execute faultlessly. Spend your time looking at the points of difference between what other companies have done successfully and what you are trying to achieve. Customize the concepts that inspire you, as needed, rather than fabricating them from scratch. Use the time saved to get to know your customers better, understand the competitive landscape, develop and harness new technology, and charismatically lead your team.

Jumpstarting BIG M

In Asia, distribution and sales ("push") often take the lead in companies' efforts to drive revenue, while marketing becomes a support process to sales, consisting primarily of the tactical implementation of promotions and communications. But just because the emphasis is on marketing with a little m, it doesn't mean the company doesn't have a strategy and that the business model isn't effective. As we have seen, there are plenty of "doer" companies that are quite successful. One way to keep your marketing and management teams' focus on aggressively implementing little m Marketing is to simply borrow a strategy and bolt it in place. Ideas for strategies that will provide a framework for the little m Marketing and also provide a rallying point for your team can be borrowed from another company or another business model, or imported from overseas case studies and best practice.

In the BIG M, little m Map, it is the "Mm Winners" and the "Doers" – the masters of little m Marketing – who best know the lessons of "Steal the Wheel." The "Dreamers" spend all their energy getting the strategy right conceptually, and rarely have the time or resources to make it real. Jumpstart the BIG M and immediately refocus on little m Marketing.

In the Navigation Tools section of this book you will find marketing strategy and tactical promotion ideas that you can "steal" and make new again for your campaigns. In the rest of this chapter, we'll look at some other ways to get BIG M and little m Marketing plans moving quickly and effectively.

Make McStrategies

Without violating any intellectual property laws, you can pick up the major concepts and strategies of successful industries and businesses and start innovating at a higher level of detail than if you were to set out and build an entire business model from scratch.

Philippines-based Jollibee Foods is a good example of a company that has in many respects borrowed the BIG M proven strategy from McDonald's, Burger King, KFC and other major chains, and customized it with phenomenal success to the needs of their home market. Jollibee is a chain of quick-service restaurants. They sell burgers. They sell chicken. They have clean, bright restaurants in family-oriented shopping centers. They have a cheery character mascot in the form of a red and yellow bee.

Adapting a proven concept to consumer markets the company knows well has been a masterstroke for Jollibee. The company has tailored the international formula to meet the tastes and needs of the Asian consumer. For example, their burger is topped with pineapple. The dessert pies offer flavors such as mango and peach proven to be popular among customers in the Philippines. They use local celebrities in their advertising for local appeal. The differences are not large, but they are significant in that management has been able to focus on superior execution of the strategy, pinpointing the desires of their local customers. The company says it has taken its management inspiration from other businesses in other industries, such as Singapore Airlines, known for its efficiency, and Disney for its family atmosphere.

Although at a much earlier stage of development than McDonald's, Jollibee has opened three outlets for every McDonald's in the Philippines. The approach has worked in their home market of the Philippines, and it is hoped to be exportable as the company expands into China and even the US. Their aim is to build an initial target customer base among the overseas Filipino community, and then broaden its appeal to other groups.

Another company that has taken an international business model and tailored it for Asia is the Hong Kong-based make-it-and-sell-it clothing retailer Giordano, which has established a strong position as "The Gap of Asia" by cleverly customizing its styles and sizing, stores merchandising and price points to meet the fashion needs and value demands of their customers. Giordano is also one of only a handful of Asia's homegrown brands.

Think laterally

Lateral thinking is a powerful BIG M, little m Marketing strategy. Perhaps more than simply "stealing the wheel," this should be considered "borrowing the wheel and then turning it 90 degrees." Some examples of lateral thinking include asking yourself:

- How would executives in other business sectors handle the same problem?
- What insight can my Chief Financial Officer add to solving this marketing problem?
- What if we targeted a different customer with the same product?
- What if we targeted the same customer with a different product?
- What if our product was 50% less expensive?
- What if it was 50% more expensive?
- What materials have never been used in our industry before? Why?
- If our brand were a celebrity, who would it be? Can we hire that person?

- Where are the places you cannot find our product? Why not and how do we get it there?

- If we had the same team and distribution channels but were in a different business, what business would it be?

Lateral thinking is about breaking out of fixed ways of thinking and opening new BIG M Marketing opportunities. Many firms in Asia find training in lateral thinking to be a useful way to counterbalance the rigid cultural and hierarchical ways of thinking that some employees bring to bear on marketing challenges. Lateral thinking also allows marketing executives to use international theories and case studies as a jumping off point for their own brainstorming about how to solve problems in their own local markets. Lateral thinking does not dictate the solution, but rather generates fresh thinking that can lead to competitive advantage.

Buy licenses and components

A powerful and legal way of "stealing the wheel" is to license intellectual property and patents, or purchase technology that your company doesn't possess. Most companies are open to licensing out their technology if it brings in additional revenue and does not create potentially dangerous competitors. Most businesses create more value than they can exploit. Major international companies spend hundreds of millions of dollars on research and development. Even after the management, product development and marketing departments have wracked their brains and tested the market for just about every use of the company's technology and patents, they will inevitably miss some opportunities, or not be in a position to exploit every opportunity they have created. This is especially true in the Asia-Pacific region, where the larger multinationals generally generate around 10-15% of their worldwide revenue. If there is a crisis in the US or Europe, they tend to set Asia aside. These lapses leave the way open for others to purchase your components or license your technology to exploit new markets or market niches.

A good example of this approach is the bold move made by Malaysia's national carmaker Proton. They purchased 80% of the Lotus Group, the renowned UK sports-car company, and later increased its share to over 95%. In addition to the engineering resources and benefits that are now available to Proton, the Lotus stake has also provided Proton with a BIG M Marketing coup. They are now manufacturing and exporting a hatchback model called the Proton Satria Gti, which is branded "Engineered by Lotus." The combination of the cache of the Lotus name, and the superior road-handling performance, styling and power that Lotus provides at least allowed Proton to compete credibly in a new higher price and higher margin sector that no amount of pure little m Marketing could have achieved. Proton can also make such aspirational marketing claims as "Lotus inspired" and "handling by Lotus."

Another vintage example is Samsung's efforts in the 1970s to meet world class manufacturing standards for microwave ovens. Worldwide sales of microwave ovens jumped from 600,000 units in 1970 to 2.2 million in 1975. A team at Samsung was organized to develop an affordable, quality mass-market microwave oven. The team had no insight into the needs of the consumers for whom they were designing and the engineers were simply challenged with the task of creating a lower-cost version of name brand models. Samsung's efforts to get into this sector started in 1976, when Samsung bought samples of US-made microwave ovens such as General Electric's Jet 230 and reverse engineered them to create their own locally produced model.

Although reverse engineering the oven's casing and controls required the team to put in intensive 80-hour work weeks, they eventually replicated the components and mechanism of the case, food platter and controls. However, the actual microwave-producing magnetron at the heart of the oven proved difficult to imitate. The team could not reinvent the technology, so the initial models were shipped with magnetrons purchased from Japanese companies. Later on, a US company called Amperex (which was on its way out of business) sold its equipment to Samsung to produce the vital part.

Although in later stages of the project Samsung invested heavily to allow engineers to travel overseas to meet with consumers, the initial success was based purely on duplicating microwave-oven production at a lower cost and higher profit margin than the US brand names could deliver. Samsung began its microwave-oven business with OEM contracts with JC Penney, progressed to supplier agreements with General Electric, and culminated with Samsung-branded ovens for both domestic consumption and export sales.

In both the above cases, the focus is on the importance of the "Doers" since the strategies are borrowed from other markets. Until the market is more fully developed, BIG M Marketing will probably not be effective.

Next time you face a marketing challenge, before you try to solve it, stop and think through a detailed description of what the problem is. Try to define the situation in the broadest way possible and look at how other marketers in other industries or other countries may have solved the same problem. Then "steal the wheel!"

Navigation Tools

Making progress every day

7
Navigation Tools

So, marketing in Asia is a journey. The intrepid traveler is steered by a Compass. The True North of BIG M Marketing is clear and present. Its polar opposite, little m Marketing tactical execution, is inextricably linked and well defined. You have a Map, with all the coordinates from Winners to Dreamers and Duds to Doers laid out. You know the lay of the land, the social, economic and historical terrain of the Asian marketing landscape. There are Eight Signposts to Success discovered along the way. Each offers reassurance that the marketer is at least headed on the right path, and offers direction and anecdotes from previous travelers along the way.

What else does the marketer in Asia need? Besides, of course, luck, and we've covered that already. For the sophisticated marketer and the novice alike there is a large array of navigation tools available, which help fill in the blind spots, cut corners and guide the marketer out of blind alleys. Just about every course has been steered before and just about every trail traversed, albeit in a different time or for a different brand, or a different company. The marketer can become more successful by learning from the colossal mistakes and even greater successes of the past, as well as accessing some tools, techniques, resources and checklists that are specifically relevant to what the needs are in Asia today. This last section of the book provides some navigation tools for the Asian marketer to borrow, steal, adapt, or be inspired by.

BIG M, little m Marketing Orienteering

BIG M, little m Marketing Orienteering is a step-by-step qualitative analytical process that works at a variety of levels to help companies understand:

- how effective their marketing strategies are;
- how effective their marketing tactics are;
- how well coordinated the strategies and tactics are;
- where the company lies on the BIG M, little m Marketing Map;
- what direction the company is moving and how fast;
- what steps need to be taken to assure BIG M, little m Marketing success;

BIG M, little m Marketing Orienteering is flexible and versatile and can be used either rigorously or on an ad hoc basis to help with evaluation. On a more casual basis, Orienteering can be used to help set the agenda for a meeting, with the participants quickly roughing out the Map on the whiteboard and using it as a guide for use throughout the conversation. Alternatively, Orienteering can be used in a more disciplined way as a quarterly review tool to determine the company's strategic positioning, to evaluate progress made between reviews and to identify potential opportunities and weaknesses. Plot your competitors on the Map as well so you have legitimate points of reference for your planning process. At its most intensive application, Orienteering can be distilled into a quantifiable checklist of parameters that are plotted and measured on a regular basis so that the placement on the Map is founded in more precise metrics. Like most business tools, it is a useful concept for management thinking on one level, and the process has the potential to yield much more meaningful results if the company is willing to put the resources against consistently gathering and plotting data points.

BIG M, little m Marketing Orienteering is applicable to:

- CEOs looking for a way to capture the big picture and competitive set
- senior management teams looking for specific indicators of market opportunity or weakness
- marketing departments as a regular diagnostic and planning tool
- individual campaigns within the overall marketing strategy
- individual marketing managers within the department

At its most sophisticated, Orienteering is a multi-tiered exercise that is built up from a series of detailed analyses, all using the same Map format, which are fed into the preparation of a company-wide summary. For SMEs that may not have such a rigid corporate structure, some steps in the BIG M, little m Marketing Orienteering can be skipped and the tool used by the managing director to get a clear bearing on marketing directions and issues facing the company.

ILLUSTRATION 7: Where does your company land on the BIG M, little m Marketing Map?

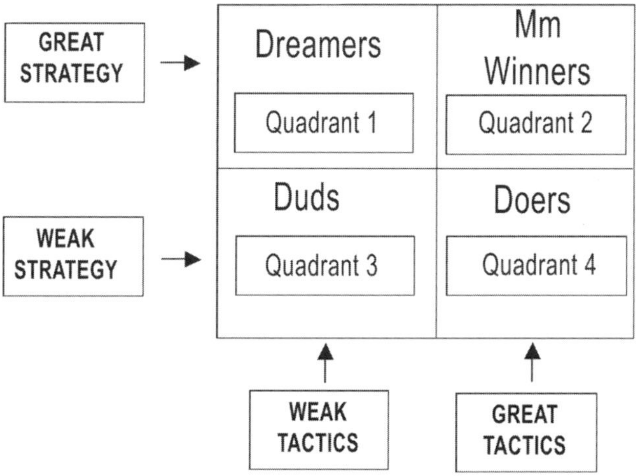

BIG M, little m Marketing Orienteering consists of five steps:

1. Gather data:
    a. On the effectiveness of your marketing strategies. What has been working? What has not? Why? To what extent can this be quantified to help with the "plotting" on the vertical axis?

    b. On your marketing tactics. Look at wholesale and sell-through rates vs. industry norms. Look at your own business performance against your budgets. Examine research data for evidence of increasing brand power, mind share and relevance to your target market.

2. Plot the results on each axis.

3. Determine where you are on the Map:
    a. in absolute terms
    b. vs. your plan
    c. vs. your competitors
    d. vs. the last measurement period.

4. Next, look at the direction in which you are moving, and how fast.

5. Assess and determine next steps.

Make an overall assessment

In addition to the rather subjective process outlined above for determining in which quadrant you fall, and in which direction you are moving, and how fast, you should be sure to evaluate the results of the Orienteering in the wider context of your company's or brand's development.

For example, ask yourself where you are in the product's lifecycle. If the product has been recently launched and it is early days, it is natural to expect that the BIG M Marketing is going to be further advanced and more sophisticated than the little m Marketing. There may be no immediate need to actively fix a situation that may well sort itself out as the product moves through the lifecycle. Later on in the cycle, watch out for the dangers of being overly tactical. Perhaps the brand is assumed to be strong and solid forever and the company has not taken a BIG M Marketing look at its strategy and the brand's potential in a long time. Or, perhaps, the relentless focus on little m Marketing is a way to squeeze as much profit out of the brand as it heads toward extinction. There are no right or wrong answers here, but no BIG M, little m Marketing decisions should be made without the benefit of a complete understanding of the situation.

Here are some danger signals that can flag potential problems as part of the Orienteering process. Your company's BIG M and little m Marketing mix is probably out of balance if the answer to any six of the following questions is "yes":

1. Have you lost any of your top three customers in the last six months?

2. Have you lost more than 20% of your least valued customers in the last six months?

3. Has it been more than six months since you asked your customers what they want? (For B2B a direct contact made by the CEO; for B2C, consumer research)

4. Are more than 20% of your promotions failing to meet their intended goals?

5. Has marketing in your organisation been delegated more than two layers down in the hierarchy?

6. Have you won less than 15% of the last business development projects you have pitched?

7. Was your last industry award more than a year ago?

8. Are you getting less than your "share of voice" in media coverage of your industry?

9. Did you fail to meet the objectives of your last annual business plan?

10. Is your business growth coming from price discounting?

11. Are you contracting in an industry sector that is expanding?

12. Did you lose market share last year or maintain previous share levels in a growing market?

13. Is your business plan missing specific sections on the impact of the Internet and WTO in China and Taiwan?

14. Do fewer than 60% of your sales people know what the company strategy is?

BIG M Marketing Tools – The Keys to Competitive Advantage

The first step toward BIG M Marketing is for a company to become aware of the importance of strategic planning and make sure they have access to right people and resources, either within the organization, or on a consulting basis. For multinational FMCG companies, this is second nature whether they are operating in Sandusky, Ohio or Lombok, Indonesia. For many Asia-based companies, however, their initial growth and success may well have sprung from an entirely different source than strategic market planning. For example, control of prime real estate is a good base from which to grow a retail business that has little to do with strategy or planning. A number of retailers in Asia started as property owners or commercial property specialists who saw the margin opportunities of being their own tenants and collecting both rent and profits from their ventures.

Perhaps a food company grew because of market demand, and simply by answering the insistent needs of its clientele, grew to gain critical mass in the marketplace. An airline might have begun because of the bravado and flying abilities of the founders, rather than an analysis of market needs. In other cases, businesses have flourished because governments have granted monopoly status to telecommunications providers, or made trading conditions (taxes, regulations) so lenient that the industry could do nothing but flourish.

In free and competitive markets, however, the strategic market planning process takes on ever increasing importance. BIG M Marketing requires you to look critically at both the internal and external factors for success that need to be mastered, and to plan against the most promising opportunities. The process starts with identifying the goals for the entire company, and then further breaks those goals down to a set of objectives and expectations for every product, service, and business unit. Next follows an assessment of the overall environment in which the company is operating, and the competitive framework. The BIG M Marketer must then look back inside the company and determine what the strengths are and in which sectors of business it is most likely to be successful.

This section goes through the steps to BIG M Marketing strategy development one at a time and then provides a "toolbox" of methodologies and creative ideas to help you "steal the wheel" from other successful marketers.

The Strategy Crossroads

It's really hard to beat the ancient marketing lesson about the 4 Ps needed for marketing success:

- Product
- Price
- Packaging
- Promotion

It's simple, clear, and it works. If all these factors are working correctly for your consumer, then you'll have a winning strategy. Over the years, people have tried tacking on additional "P's" such as Public Affairs, and Personalization to the list, and it still works. A reminder of the 4 Ps is a useful checklist for BIG M Marketing strategy development, but so much has been written on the topic that this book will move on to look at other tools that will help with strategy development.

Plotting a marketing strategy requires looking at your business challenge from two perspectives:

- From inside your company looking outwards.
- From the customers' perspective looking inwards at your product or service (in the worse case, your potential customer *not* even looking at your product!).

The results of these two planning processes must meet and mesh at "the strategy crossroads." If they do not meet initially, either the company's marketing plans or even its product offering must be changed or the targeted customer profile needs to be changed to suit the company's offering.

Here's a checklist for devising *company outwards* marketing strategies:

- What turnover goals do you have to meet to achieve profit (sales targets)?
- What are your strongest products and services? Why?
- What are your company's strengths in product distribution? Why?
- Can your product be made cheaper and/or better than the competition?
- Do you have the capacity to meet demand?
- Who are the best professionals on your team and what are their strengths?
- What campaigns have worked well in the past?
- What are the competitors doing that you are not? Why?
- What are you doing that the competitors aren't? Why not?
- What are your weak points?
- What else is going on in your company (mergers, downsizing, IPO)?

Here is a checklist for devising *customer inwards* marketing strategies:

- What do I need this product to do?
- What do I want it to do?
- What would be the ideal product if price were no object?

- What is my budget?
- What are my choices in the marketplace?
- What is the main reason for picking one company's product over another's?
- What does this purchase compete with for my "share of wallet" (leisure, groceries, travel)?
- How do I prefer to shop (mall, village stores, Internet)?
- Where do I go to buy these particular items?
- What is important to me in my life (work, family, money, safety)?
- What packaging is most convenient and eye-catching?

When these questions are answered, the beginnings of two strategic approaches should begin to take shape quickly. Before much time or attention is spent on developing either one, look at them both together and see how they fit and where they don't. Take the best aspects of both and look for the strategy crossroads that fits both your company's strengths and the customer's needs. This BIG M strategy will then later also have to be meshed with the little m tactical plan.

The BIG M Toolbox

It is useful to take a look inside the BIG M Marketing Toolbox and see what resources are available to the marketer in Asia and why to date they have not been deployed as frequently or aggressively as possible. One of the most useful tools, which is generally underused in Asia, is positioning.

Positioning

What is the sustainable competitive position for your company, and (at the next level) your company's products? Many companies that began as monopolies, or are based upon privileged patronage never stop to even consider their positioning. They are what they have become, and for many dominant Asia-based companies and established multinationals the time has come to take a careful and objective look at competitive positioning.

In the dotcom era, companies became almost obsessive about their "elevator pitches" – the succinct company descriptions that summed up quickly and accurately (briefly enough for an elevator ride) what the company does and why it is unique and viable. At the opposite end of the scale, most companies in Asia have not spent nearly enough management time or effort on positioning. One of the most immediately useful positioning tools is the brand pyramid that is based on the work of humanist psychologist Abraham Maslow's hierarchical theory of human needs. Maslow is perhaps best known for his phrase "self-actualization," referring to people who had reached the highest level of consciousness, wisdom and creativity.

Maslow's theory looks at human motivations and behavior *after* people have met their basic needs of securing food and shelter. The fundamental functional motivations are overlayered in modern society by more sophisticated rationale and emotional needs. In a branding context, that means the marketer must find a positioning that satisfies the customer's higher needs rather than just the functional. At the top of the brand pyramid is the fully-functioning positioning equivalent of self-actualization.

ILLUSTRATION 8

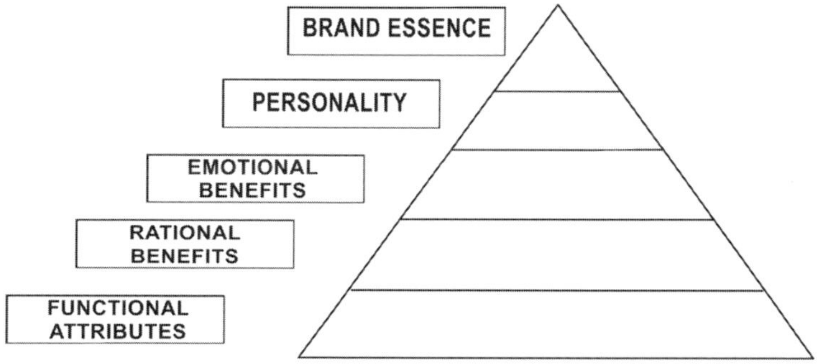

For example, if you are looking for a positioning for a brand of liquid disinfectant, clearly the product cleans surfaces and kills germs at a functional level. Up the pyramid a bit further, the disinfectant makes the home more sanitary, and at the top of the brand pyramid, the true value of the product may be giving the consumer the reassurance that they have done everything possible to create a safe, hygienic environment for their family's well-being. Many companies and brands in Asia stop their positioning exercise at the level of determining the rational and functional attributes of their products and services. Carefully mapping out a brand pyramid all the way to the top, and integrating all marketing activities around the brand benefit creates powerful long-term benefits and competitive advantage.

The essence of the positioning can come from any number of "ownable" attributes of the company, including such options as:

- Positioning on specific product features - e.g. overnight delivery or fastest microchip processor speed.

- Positioning on benefits - e.g. money-saving, faster, or more energy efficient.

- Positioning for a specific use - e.g. direct marketing or retail industries.

- Positioning for user category - e.g. the publishing industry.

- Positioning benchmarking against another product or a competing business - e.g. Procter & Gamble or Sony.

- Product class disassociation - e.g. "an airline that's more like a five star hotel."

- Hybrid bases - Incorporates elements from several types of positioning.

Even just a half-day positioning workshop with senior management executives can help to determine what positioning works best for a company. In addition, the time spent together working on a common problem builds cross-functional teamwork and strengthens company culture. Exercises such as SWOT analyses have become increasingly prevalent in Asia as more companies list on their local stock exchanges or on overseas boards, but positioning is still a vastly under-used resource.

Here's a quick look at some other useful tools for marketers in Asia to help set their BIG M Marketing direction.

Market research

Hire qualified, objective consultants to give you an external view of your customers, market share and trends. Often companies are so busy measuring the results of their little m Marketing tactics and trying to draw quantitative conclusions from their efforts that they forget (or don't want to allocate marketing budgets for) research. In many cultures executives do not feel comfortable turning to outside consultants for objective input on strategic matters, preferring instead to operate on a "command-and-control" model.

Portfolio analysis

What products and services do you offer and why? Are these the right products? Is this the right mix? Do they fit well together and help build the brand and market position beyond the efforts of the individual product teams? Many Asia companies are based on the trading model and have grown topsy-turvy with a group of barely related products and services that span more industry sectors than one company could possibly succeed in simultaneously.

Benchmarking

What are the highest standards for your industry and who sets them? How do you compare against the leaders? What are best practices for various professional disciplines? The leader in shipping and logistics in the region may not even be in your industry, but you should benchmark against the leaders. All too often in Asia, companies focus on identifying and copying other companies' systems. This can be effective, but it is not true benchmarking.

Market segmentation

Who are your different current and prospective customer groups and how do their needs differ? How should you tailor or redirect your marketing message to reach different segments of the marketplace? A market survey report "Marketing in South East Asia" conducted by High-Tech Associates, in conjunction with *AdAsia*, and The Chartered Institute of Marketing, found that while companies in Asia expect a significant share of business from existing customers, many do not differentiate their messages for new and existing customers.

Thirty six percent of the companies surveyed don't even bother to differentiate between the source of sales – whether new sales come from incremental sales to existing customers, or to new customers. Of the 64% of the companies surveyed that said they do make this differentiation, 60% predict that they will get 40% of their sales from existing customers. A smaller group (20% of companies surveyed) expect that they will get as much as 80% of their sales from existing customers. Probing further, 62% of the companies said they plan their marketing activities with both existing and new customers in mind, and 38% said that the same marketing messages apply to both existing and new customers. Clearly there is a lot of scope for better targeting to maximize the incremental sales value of existing customers, and of reaching new customers by having more sophisticated and precise messaging strategies.

Strategy in a box

Most BIG M Marketing strategies that work are marked by their simplicity. The easier a strategy is to understand, the easier it is to communicate throughout your organisation, and to execute. Although there are virtually as many strategies as there are tactics to implement them, most marketing strategies somehow involve carving out an "ownable niche" that can be built upon and protected against the onslaught from competitors. Additionally, marketing strategies are built from a relatively limited range of options which, when applied across hundreds of countries, thousands of categories and millions of individual products, creates the variety and depth of possible strategies. Here is a checklist of some common BIG M Marketing building blocks. The list isn't comprehensive – it's designed to help you brainstorm and develop the right strategy for your company, brand or product.

Early adopters

Precisely select one or two groups of people that are likely to lead opinions and influence the opinions and purchasing choices of the broader market. "Early adopters" are those consumers who have to have the newest, best product first. They are well versed on a certain sector, and know exactly what they want and why. They probably know more about your company and your competitors than your own market research tells you. By going deep to understand their needs and to trial drive among these groups, you can gain valuable consumer feedback and get a foothold amongst a group that will influence the entire market. Targeting this group will "seed" the market and help build sales via word of mouth. "Hip" teens, computer game aficionados, electronic gadget freaks and car enthusiasts all fall into this category.

Emotional/patriotic appeal

Wrap yourself in the flag. This strategy is particularly appropriate if you make a special point of doing all your manufacturing in the countries where you do business, generating employment and tax revenue for the government. For example, Dick Smith, the evergreen entrepreneur from Australia, has made a major BIG M Marketing push with his efforts to package locally made food products under the Dick Smith label to promote the fact that they are all "made in Australia" and thus deserve to be taking market share from the multinational brands that dominate Australian supermarket shelves. Dick Smith has had previous successes with his consumer electronics stores and in the aviation industry, and personally carries with him the aura of Australian business success so he is highly credible when he wraps his business in the flag.

Another brand that wraps itself in the Australian flag is Foster's beer, and this marketing approach has proved successful overseas. At home in Australia, however, Foster's is not among the major brands.

This strategy is not limited to just patriotism, there are many other deep-seated emotions to which marketers can appeal. Cause-related marketing in which consumers are drawn to make a purchase because a certain percentage of the profits are allocated to a charitable cause is another emotional strategy. Sometimes an emotional or patriotic appeal is exactly what a mundane business driven by little m Marketing needs to lift the customer's interest and sales.

Concentration strategy

Pick one segment of the market and go for it wholeheartedly. For example, target teens in a way that is completely in their own language and culture. Skechers footwear, JNCO jeans, and Quiksilver's Roxy apparel have all built growing brands worldwide off this strategy. You may turn off 80% of the total customer universe, but you will own the other 20% solidly. In fact, the more you turn off your non-target group, the more you will turn on the core group.

Guerilla marketing

Jump outside usual advertising and promotional channels and reach your target customer in an arresting and compelling way. For example, when your competitor sponsors a major high-visibility sporting event, surround that event with eye-catching events and product placements featuring your brand and your product. Do it so creatively and completely that the consumers are confused as to who the real sponsor is. You may end up in a better position by using guerilla marketing than if you had invested in the event sponsorship fees. Guerilla marketing is not for everyone or every company, and certainly is not for the faint of heart because the potential for failure is high. However, the use of guerilla marketing has not been a traditional BIG M Marketing strength in Asia, and the future is wide open for companies willing to seize this inroad to competitive advantage.

Turn the tables

This strategy relies on behaving in ways that reverse the customer's expectations. For example, are you operating in a low status, low price, and low margin sector? Surprise the market by suddenly switching to a premium positioning. This approach is described in the "Move Upstream" section as shocking the price value equation. Of course you will also have to make operational changes to support the luxury position, such as customer service, packaging, choice of advertising media and quality of manufacturing. However, once the BIG M strategy is determined, the little m tactical plan virtually writes itself.

Other ideas to turn the tables include:

- Where would the consumer never expect to see your product? Put it there!
- What if you eliminated the feature customers like best and replaced it with something else?
- Can you reposition a men's product for women? Women's for men?
- What two product categories have never been combined before? For example, would there be a market for a combination car wash and beauty salon where patrons were coiffed while their vehicles were washed?
- Can you take a scary or boring segment and make it fun? (e.g. insurance)
- Shake loose people's ideas of what consumers want, when or where. How about Coca-Cola for breakfast, or selling real estate to people stuck in Bangkok traffic jams?
- Less is more. What should you stop doing that everyone else is doing?

One-price policy

Cut through all your industry's cluttered pricing issues by offering the same product to everyone at the same price everywhere. For example, in a wholesale food business, you may turn off some of your best, high-volume distributor customers who are used to getting special deals, but you may make up any lost volume and more by instituting a simple, clear pricing policy. You will also save management time, which can be reallocated to BIG M Marketing strategy rather than administrating a complex system. This strategy is also seen in those shops where all items, regardless of type, are the same price. The all-you-can-eat buffet is another variation. Would this approach work in your industry?

Borrow interest

This strategy is the essence of all sponsorship. If your target customer doesn't care about your company or your product, how can you get their attention and show you are relevant? Some ideas include:

- celebrity sponsorship
- give away a million dollars
- look for a sex appeal angle (even if the link is not obvious)
- link with a club or industry association
- tie-in with music.

If you think your customer isn't going to be interested in your product or service, or at least not now, borrow some interest to spark awareness and sales. This strategy can also provide a differentiating factor between one brand and another where perhaps there is none integral to the actual product.

Line extension

If they like it as a washing-up powder, they'll love it as a car wax; or maybe not! Line extensions should be approached with caution. If your brand is strong and you are in a market sector that is mature and has limited scope for growth, putting your brand on other products can be an effective BIG M Marketing strategy. Line extensions can present additional marketing opportunities, but if they fail, they can prove detrimental to the parent brand.

Superior service

Use customer service as the "X factor" to differentiate your product or service in the marketplace. The world certainly doesn't need another dry cleaner, but what if you could give 30-minute service with free door-to-door delivery?

Among the leaders in *Media* magazine's 2002 Asian Brands Poll are companies that stress service as their hallmarks and have carved out strong market positions for themselves, such as Shangri-La hotels (#2 in brand familiarity with 81% of respondents saying they know it very well, and #1 in quality), Mandarin Oriental hotels (#6 in overall brand familiarity), Peninsula hotels (# 8 in brand familiarity), and Singapore Airlines (#4 in brand familiarity, # 2 as a visionary brand, #2 as "here for the long term" and #2 in innovative brands). As *Media* magazine points out, these companies' service standards, helped by low labor costs in the region, have allowed them to build a point of difference in the increasingly commoditised travel marketplace.

These are just a few examples of strategies that can be borrowed, twisted and shifted to fit whatever the situation demands. You can also get inspiration from looking at other company's strategies from other industries and look for ways to adapt their strengths to your industry.

little m Marketing Toolbox

Once you have your BIG M Marketing strategy in place, the selection and integration of the right little m Marketing tactics becomes critical. As one of the Signposts to Success says: "Steal the Wheel!" This section of the book provides a selection of tools and resources to help you swiftly and effectively pull together the tactical aspects of your marketing campaign without having to reinvent the wheel.

The answer is "New, Now, Win, and Free"

Whatever the marketing question, in just about every situation at least one of the answers is "New", "Now", "Win", or "Free." These are the four most powerful words in marketing, although arguably "Sex" should be added to the list. Can you think of any more powerful way to get a jaded consumer's attention than to offer "New: Win free sex now?" Just about any little m Marketing campaign can be traced back to one of these concepts in one way or another. You can look longer or think harder about coming up with promotional ideas, but often it's most effective to keep it simple and basic. How can you work with these four basic, proven concepts? For example:

New

- New model
- New and improved
- Limited edition
- Latest technology

Now

- Added benefit for acting now
- Meet an immediate need (at the gym: "Thirsty for water now?")

Win

- The holiday of your dreams
- A million dollars

- A year's groceries
- You may have already won
- Potential customer benefit beyond the product or service
- Reason to interact with the company (and share information)

Free

- No-risk trial period
- Your first one is free
- Two for one offer
- Buy 10 get one free
- Customer loyalty "air miles" program
- Bundle premium and lesser value items into a package

The tactics bank

If it's been thought of before out there, it's probably in here. Here's a comprehensive list of little m Marketing concepts that you can steal, improve on, combine, and refresh. Whether brainstorming by yourself or in a group, you will find your thinking is faster and clearer when you don't have to re-create the basics each time. Pick a topic and dive right in. Run through the lists and see what is relevant to your marketing situation and challenge. You'll find many of the ideas may be inappropriate or irrelevant, but after you've filtered through the whole catalogue, you will be left with a core group of concepts that are worth developing further. You'll get there faster than if you tried to explore all the possibilities from scratch. And, you can save your brainpower for the BIG M!

They are grouped by type of idea and then alphabetically so try mixing and matching for fresh combinations.

Locations	Media	Other
airport lounge	advertising	backgrounder
art gallery	aerial sign writing	balloons
bank	article reprint	before/after photograph video
bus	bank ATM message	biggest-ever
caravan	bill board poster	board game
college	book	calendar
customs house	brand	cartoon strip
dance theatre	break a Guinness record	children and pets
embassy	building image projection	Chinese new year promotion
factory tour	bus/ferry/train	convention
fashion show	cartoon picture book	costume event
gallery	case study	customer survey
harbour	celebrity endorsement	database research
helicopter trip	comedy skit	dealer tie-in
history museum	competition	design contest
hospital	dance	dinner
Imax theatre	demonstration	direct marketing
junk	ferry race	disaster relief
library	fireworks	discount
movie studio	flight	e-mail campaign
museum	go-kart race	educational wall
national park	golf pro am	environmental awareness
office building	hot air balloon	face of the year
police station	Internet chat line campaign	feng shui tie-in
roadshow	intranet issue website	financial report
schools		focus group
stadium		golf day
technology park		graphic illustrations
temple		hologram
theatre		hotline to management
university		information bureau
zoo		informational manual
		industry association

BIG M, little m Marketing Integration Check

The BIG M, little m Marketing integration check is a qualitative tool to help you determine whether you have the right mix of strategies and tactics. The key is to:

Triangulate: top down, bottom up, and from outside.

Get a fix on the innovations your company's marketing needs by "triangulating" your assessment. Go through the exercise of looking at your marketing as objectively as possible from three different viewpoints: strategy down; tactics up; and customer in. Start anywhere you like in the process, but gather three distinct perspectives on what you are doing and what you could be doing. Capture all your thoughts (or do this as a marketing team "whiteboard" group exercise).

ILLUSTRATION 9
Where Bottom Up and Top Down Meet

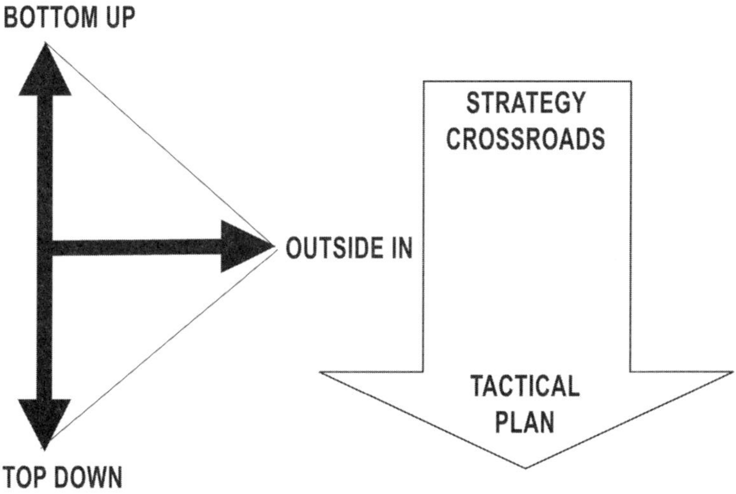

Top down

Pretend your strategy is set in stone and cannot be changed. Against that strategy, what tactics are working best? Which ones need improvement or replacing? Write them down and move on to an assessment of the tactics.

Bottom up

Look at all the tactics you are using that really work. Now set aside whatever strategies you already have in place, and brainstorm some "blue sky" strategies that fit these tactics. You may find you need more or other tactics to achieve the hypothetical strategies. That's OK. Write down a list of effective tactics, possible new strategies, and desirable new tactics.

Outside in

Now put yourself in your customer's and the competitor's shoes. How has the customer's need shifted since the last time you made an assessment? Is the strategy still right? Do the tactics still seem fresh and effective? Perhaps the market has grown more crowded, customers have become more sophisticated, or more jaded. Record your thoughts and observations. What should stay and what should go? You should also conduct objective research among your customers to make sure you are making decisions based on real data, not just what you think they may think.

Then, use the three points of triangulation to map out where you are and where you have to go to integrate your strategies and tactics. You will find many insights in various combinations, such as:

- All three perspectives tell you to start (or stop) doing the same things.
- Your tactics are working by themselves but don't support your strategy.
- Your tactics don't work. Is it time for a new strategy, or better tactics?
- Your customers are unhappy and the finger is pointed at your strategy.
- Your customers are happy, but your business is not meeting its targets.

All too often in Asia, marketers do not triangulate before making decisions that have tremendous implications for their businesses. At the risk of over generalizing, there is a tendency to change the strategy when the tactics aren't working. If early milestones are missed, rather than staying the course with a potentially successful strategy that just needs more time or better tactical execution, a new strategy will be implemented. This phenomenon is especially evident among the trading and distribution companies. This confusion of BIG M and little m Marketing must be avoided at all costs and triangulation is a good way to stay on course.

See what the Rest of the World is Doing

Here's a rundown of marketing-related website resources the author has found useful at work and in the research for this book. Surf the marketing turf in Asia and around the world for ideas and inspiration!

About Management	www.management.about.com
AsianBusiness	www.Asianbusinessnet.com
Asia Internet.com	www.Asia.internet.com
Asia Society	www.Asiasource.com
Biz Report Network	www.bizreport.com
Brand Channel	www.brandchannel.com
Branding Asia	www.brandingasia.com
Brand News	www.brandera.com
Booz-Allen's "strategy plus business"	www.strategy-business.com
Business 2.0 Magazine	www.business2.com
CIA Factbook	www.odci.gov/cia/publications/factbook/index/html
Cluetrain Manifesto	www.cluetrain.com
Customers.com	www.customers.com
DK World Desk Reference	www.travel.dk.com/wdr/
dnm Strategies	www.dnmstrategies.com
Edward de Bono/lateral thinking	www.edwdebono.com
Far Eastern Economic Review	www.feer.com
Google.com	www.google.com

Gorilla Asia	www.gorillasia.com
Harvard Business School Publishing	www.hbsp.harvard.edu
High Tech Associates	www.hightech.com.sg
Idea Site For Business	www.ideasiteforbusiness.com/ideas.htm
Interbrand	www.interbrand.com
Library of Congress Country Studies	http://lcweb2.loc.gov/frd/cs/cshome.html
Media & Marketing	www.media.com.hk
Red Herring magazine	www.redherring.com
The Seybold Group	www.psgroup.com
Sookoo Business Strategy Search Specialist	www.sookoo.com
Thunderbird Graduate School of International Management	www.t-bird.edu
Upstream Asia	www.Upstream Asia.com
Wharton School's Center for Leadership and Change Management	http://leadership.wharton.upenn.edu
Wired Magazine	www.wired.com
World Economic Forum	www.weforum.org
ManagementFirst	www.managementfirst.com
University of Hawaii/Aspy P. Palia	www.cba.Hawaii.edu/aspy/aspymktr.htm
World Trade Organization	www.wto.org

Afterword

"The art of certain victory, the mode of harmonizing with changes, is a matter of opportunity ... And of all avenues of seeing opportunity, none is greater than the unexpected."

- Zhuge Liang,
  Records of the
  Loyal Lord of
  Warriors

"While man makes plans, the outcome depends on heaven."

- Chinese proverb

Afterword

Since this is a book about change and continuous navigation towards an ever-shifting objective, there really is no conclusion. Like any guidebook author, I'm not about to say, "Well, I told you where to go and what to do. Don't screw it up!" Instead, I do hope you enjoy the journey as much as I do, and find it profitable.

Many of the dynamics of Asia's BIG M, little m Marketing have been identified, and some winning strategies and effective tactics have been shared, but the plain fact is that you have to find your own way. Marketplaces continuously evolve as social, political and economic environments change; as customers become more savvy and demanding; and as marketers become ever more responsive and sophisticated. Ultimately you, the reader, as well as the companies in Asia, their customers, government officials, the media, accountants, historians, and maybe even the fortune tellers, will have a hand in recording the ongoing conclusion.

BIG M, little m Marketing is not a compendium of pat answers to common regional branding and sales problems; instead it provides a framework to help determine the right marketing strategy in conjunction with the right marketing tactics. Doing great BIG M, little m Marketing is about asking the right questions at the right time. You may finish off with more questions than solutions, but you need to act now to put the issues that face your company, your brand, your product and, yes, also your career into sharp relief. Would you rather be known for panicking and fleeing from a problem, or for discovering a way forward and being responsible for profitably managing the response to a situation that is threatening the business?

As we approach the end of *BIG M, little m Marketing*, let's go back to the beginning and look at the implications of some of the trends and changes sweeping the Asia region in the context of your own situation. Whether you are a student, an Asia-based executive, an international marketer, or indeed a government official overseeing the emerging marketing environment, take a minute to see how and where *you* fit in.

Here are fourteen questions to ask yourself (as a professional, as a manager, and as a company executive in this changing environment). These match up with the changes and trends identified at the beginning of the book for those who would like to have an unfair advantage. Actually, there are no right or wrong answers, and sorry folks, this isn't the class Asian Marketing 101 quiz, so sometimes the answers are even less clear than the questions. But, the unanswered questions might provide more insight and direction than you had foreseen at the beginning of this book, and that in and of itself should be worthwhile. And, to make it more challenging (seeing as all the answers are at the very least hinted at throughout the book), there are some thought-provoking follow-up questions (no extra credit granted).

1. Do you make (or have you made) a sacrifice in revenue or profit today for a longer term international growth return tomorrow?

   Follow-up question: When was the last time you spent more than half a day a week thinking about business outside your specific geographic or profit center area?

2. Is your day-to-day business based on sales (customer) relationships or business partnerships?

   Follow-up question: How many of your current customers would follow you to a new company if you switched jobs? How many of your customers would remain if your company switched to doing business in a different industry sector?

3. Name three people whom you could call in for a favor right now to expand distribution by 20% or make incremental sales of 10%.

   Follow-up question: If the answer was "zero" could you help build the business to those levels within one year without anyone's help?

4. Is there someone in government or at an industry association you could call tomorrow to help you stop a slide in your company's sales?

Follow-up question: Who would you contact if you felt your company was being victimized by non-competitive practices?

5. Name two international trends or management theories that have added value to your business?

   Follow-up question: Take a look through the current issues of *Harvard Business Review*, *Business Week* and *Fortune* magazine. Can you find any business strategy or approach that does not work in *Asia*? Why?

6. Are you part of an entrenched business that has an extensive network of partners and government contacts?

   Follow-up question: If not, why not? (Joke.) Real question: What aspects of your competitive advantage may be eroding and need to be replaced in the coming five years?

7. Do you vertically control and implement more than 75% of your business from manufacturing to sales?

   Follow-up question: What percentage of your business is outsourced? Of that amount, how much is manufacturing and how much is IT services or business processes?

8. Are you satisfying 95% of your customers 95% of the time?

   Follow-up question: Have you discovered the efficiencies of mass customization (Marks and Spencer) or are you still tailoring special clothes for every customer?

9 Is your business tied in with a company or individual that can get positive messages about your product or service in the media?

   Follow-up question: If you don't have such connections, how do you get yourself heard and how can you work with the media to help you gain competitive advantage?

10. Are you connected to, or do you have access to, one of Asia's ruling businesses or government families?

    Follow-up question: Do you have a solid CRM program in place to identify customer needs and satisfy them profitably?

11. Do you know exactly who your customers are and what they want?

    Follow-up question: What is the last thing a customer told *you*?

12. Do you consider your current advertising and sales promotion campaign successful?

    Follow-up question: What will your customer want in two years?

13. Do you have all the orders you need or can handle through your distribution channels?

    Follow-up question: What if my current sales network was wiped out? What alternative or more efficient ways are available to sustain your business?

14. If you are a Harvard Business School graduate, rich, and a nephew of the mayor of Shanghai, why do you still need BIG M little m Marketing?

    Follow-up question: Your uncle just died. Now what do you do?

Your answers to these questions will help determine your ability to cope or even thrive in the increasingly competitive marketing environment. Despite the deep roots in tradition and culture of many business practices, they are not immutable. Evolutionary economic and social changes are sweeping across Asia and momentum is gaining for reformation and transformation of the way business is done in the region. As the rigidity and cronyism that has typified business in Asia begins to be replaced by transparency and a more level playing field, the potential opens up for business people to release tremendous marketing power.

As we have seen, the little m Marketing tactics that helped carry many companies and Asian economies through their formative years will have to be augmented by BIG M strategies going forward to survive and achieve competitive advantage.

If you take nothing else away with you from this book and the BIG M, little m Marketing concept, I do hope you have learned some questions to ask yourself and your colleagues and business partners, even if you haven't the answers. As you work with BIG M, little m Marketing and apply some of the business ideas to your own enterprises, I would like to hear how they work, and to know the lessons learned from your experience (e-mail david@upstreamasia.com). Since we're writing the conclusion together, perhaps they could even make it into a future edition of *BIG M, little m Marketing*, in the "Mm Winners" section, hopefully!

Endnotes

Companies/organizations mentioned in this book

Amazon.com	www.amazon.com
Amway	www.amway.com
Acer	www.acer.com
Ajinomoto	www.ajinomoto.com
Ariba	www.ariba.com
Astra International	www.astra.co.id
Batey Ads	www.bateyads.com.sg
Boeing	www.boeing.com
Bossini	www.bossini.com.hk
Burson-Marsteller*	www.bm.com
Café de Coral	www.cafedecoral.com
Calvin Klein*	
Carrefour	www.carrefour.com
Cathay Pacific	www.cathaypacific.com
Cerebos	www.cerebos.com
Cheung Kong	www.ckh.com
Circle K	www.circlek.com
Citroën	www.citroen.co.uk
Coca-Cola	www.cocacola.com
Colliers Jardine*	www.residential.colliers.com
Creative Technology	www.cict.co.uk
Cycle and Carriage	www.cyclecarriage.com.sg
Dell	www.dell.com
Dick Smith	www.dse.com.au
DoCoMo	www.nttdocomo.com
ebabyasia*	www.ebabyasia.com
eBay*	www.ebay.com
EDS	www.eds.com
Edward Keller*	www.edwardkeller.com
Ford Motor	www.ford.com
Fuji	www.fujifilm.com
GAP	www.gap.com
Gateway Computer	www.gateway.com
General Electric	www.ge.com
General Motors*	www.gm.com
Giant	www.giant-bicycle.com
Global Sources	www.globalsources.com
Good Enough	
Google	www.google.com
Grant Thornton*	www.gthk.com.hk
G2000	www.g2000.com.hk
Haagen-Dazs*	www.haagen-dazs.com

Hindustan Lever	www.hll.com
Honda	www.honda.com
Hong Kong Trade Development Council	www.tdctrade.com
HSBC	www.hsbc.com
Hutchison	www.line.net
Hutchison Whampoa	www.hutchison-whampoa.com
~H2O+	www.h2oplus.com.hk
JNCO	www.jnco.com
Jollibee Foods	www.jollibee.com
Joyce Boutique	www.joyce.com
Kellogg's	www.kelloggs.com
Kentucky Fried Chicken	www.kfc.com
Kennex	www.kennex.com.hk
Kodak	www.kodaz.com
Landor	www.landor.com
Lane Crawford	www.lanecrawford.com
Legend	www.legendent.com
Lever Brothers	www.leverpakistan.com
Li & Fung	www.lifung.com
Lotus Group	www.lotusgroup.com
McDonald's*	www.mcdonalds.com
Mercedes Benz*	www.mercedes-benz.com
Microsoft MSN*	www.msn.com
New Zealand Kiwi Marketing Board (Zespri)	www.zespri.com
Nielsen//Netratings*	www.nielsennetratings.com
Nike	www.nike.com
Nokia	www.nokia.com
NuSkin	www.nuskin.com
Orange	www.orange.com
Pacific Coffee	www.2netvigator.co/ente/café/pacific/store.html
Panasonic	www.panasonic.com
Park 'n Shop	www.parknshop.com
Pedigree*	www.pedigree.com
Pepsico*	www.pepsico.com

Pohang Iron and Steel Company (Posco)	www.posco.co.kr/en
Pizza Hut*	www.pizzahut.com
Procter & Gamble*	www.pg.com
Proton	www.proton.com
Quiksilver Roxy	www.quicksilver.com
Rambus RDRAM	www.rambus.com
Reebok*	www.reebok.com
Samsung	www.samsung.com
Sanrio/Hello Kitty	www.sanrio.com
Sara Lee	www.saralee.com
Singapore Airlines	www.singaporeair.com
Skechers	www.skechers.com
Sesami, Inc	www.sesami.com
7-11	www.7-eleven.com
3M*	www.3m.com
Sony*	www.sony.com
South China Morning Post	www.scmp.com
Starbucks	www.starbucks.com
Taco Bell	www.tacobell.com
Thums Up	
Tiger Balm	www.tigerbalm.co.uk
Toyota	www.toyota.com
Tricon	www.triconglobal.com
Tupperware	www.tupperware.com
Uni-clo	www.uniqlo.com
Virgin	www.virgin.com
V-Tech	www.vtech.com
Volkswagen	www.vw.com

* indicates companies with which the author or Upstream Asia has worked directly.

Sources and Notes

Many of the anecdotes and insights in this book come directly from the author's own experience. Friends, colleagues, business associates and journalists also provided large amounts of first hand data. These people are thanked in the Acknowledgements section. In every instance, the author has made every reasonable effort to check facts and portray people, companies and events fairly and accurately. However, no reliance should be placed on the contents, and individuals should make their own independent inquiries and satisfy themselves as to the truth and accuracy of that information before taking any action.

This is not a scholarly work, and much of the information cited is commonly known and freely available on the Web, in newspapers, magazines and books. To help make the text of this book flow more easily and be readable without distraction, there are no footnotes. Where a specific author or document is cited, attribution is made in this "Sources and Notes" section under the relevant chapter heading,

BIG M, little m Marketing

Details of the "Marketing in South East Asia" report cited are included in the bibliography. Details of the "Marketing in South East Asia" survey report are included in the Bibliography.

Asian Sense and Business Sensibility

The quotation "Asia is modernizing in 'the Asia way.'" is from John Naisbitt's book *Megatrends Asia.* Quotation about Chinese originating from a common ancestor from *Sons of the Yellow Emperor*, Lynn Pan, 1990 Martin Secker & Warburg Ltd, page 12. Information on communications and context from the University of Hawaii website http://library.kcc.hawaii.edu/external/asdp/econ/Asian/barrett.html. Insight on relationships and transactions from *Business Horizons, Relationship Marketing the Chinese Way*. Author: Oliver H.M. Yau, Issue: Jan, 2000 [http://www.elsevier.com/inca/publications/store/6/2/0/2/1/4/]. Hutchison's 3G sales in the Britain example drawn from "Deutsche cool to Hutchison 3G phone sale plan," *South China Morning Post*, September 3, 2002. Background information on the "gatekeeper" inside the culture from the University of Hawaii website http://library.kcc.hawaii.edu/external/asdp/busad/Asian/mkt2350.htm. Information on management decision making found on the University of Hawaii website http://library.kcc.hawaii.edu/external/asdp/econ/Asian/barrett.html. Story of Posco and Brigadier General Park from Mark L. Clifford's *Troubled Tiger: businessmen, bureaucrats, and generals in South Korea*, pages 67-75. Implications of proprietary information: *Business Horizon, Relationship Marketing the Chinese Way*. Author: Oliver H.M. Yau, Issue: Jan, 2000. Tupperware India example from Interbrand [http://www.interbrand.com/features_profile.asp?id=37].

The Compass

Comment on importance of tactics in designing marketing campaigns from *Bottom Up Marketing*: Al Ries & Jack Trout. McGraw Hill, 1989. ISBN 0-07-052733-4

Dreamers

Overview of ADMART from *Asiaweek* magazine http://www.asiaweek.com/asiaweek/magazine/99/1203/cover1.html. Background for DuPont section from www.asiacase.com website: article abstract from Ivey Publishing [http://www.asiacase.com/full/page-PROSTRAT-70257.html]. Historical information on Pepsi, Coke and Thums Up in India from "Pepsi-Coke war propped Thums Up fortune: Unctad Report," *Press Trust of India,* Indian Express Newspapers (Bombay) Ltd, September 28, 1997 and Agencyfaqs! [http://www.agencyfaqs.com/www1/news/stories/2002/05/06/4312.html]

Mm Winners

Background on Legend for Core Pacific-Yamaichi/IDC research and Morgan Stanley Dean Witter. Information on Sanrio Hello Kitty drawn from Wired Magazine and Interbrand [http://www.wired.com/wired/archive/9.09/topten_pr.html and http://www.interbrand.com/features_profile.asp?id=9] respectively.

Duds

Malaysia's Abdullah Badawi comments on cronyism from *Far Eastern Economic Review* interview, August 2002.

Water Oasis: source interviews with MD Salina Yu.

BIG M, little m Companies In Asia Today

Information on Konka drawn from *Emerging Chinese MNCs: Konka Group Company Limited* by Professor Biswatosh Saha, Vinod Gupta School of Management at Indian Institute of Technology Kharagpur, India. See bibliography for details.

Interbrand brand value survey information from Interbrand Corp., *Business Week* and J.P. Morgan Chase & Co. 2002, as reported in *Business Week*'s August 5, 2002 issue, which also provided the US$ 200 million Samsung advertising budget figure [http://bwnt.businessweek.com/brand/2002/index.asp]. ImagePower Survey information found at the Landor Associates website www.landor.com. Asian Brands Poll 2002 information from *Media* magazine, August 2002. From kiwi fruit to Zespri: Interbrand [http://www.interbrand.com/features_profile.asp?id=28]. Quotation from Alexander Kojeve about the "Japanization of the West" from *Turning Japanese (Japanese influence on Western culture)*: Robert Gray. Issue Sept 21, 2000. Information on China's most valuable brands: *People's Daily,* Dec. 18, 2001. Information on Lucky film from the World Economic Forum website [www.weforum.com] – notes from 2000 China Business Summit, April 18, 2000.

Trends and the Future

Data on outsourcing from the IDC report *Asia IT Outsourcing Market & Trends, 1999-2004*. Information on US/China trade balance from US Department of Commerce statistics and the US-China Business Council. Comment from Ford's Wayne Booker, World Economic Forum, China Business 2000 Report. China's Emerging Global Role: Impact, Opportunities and Challenges, Beijing 16-18 April 2000. [www.weforum.org/pdf/SummitReports/china2000.pdf]. Statistics on Taiwan's SMEs from *Republic of China Yearbook 2001*, Government Information Office [http://www.gio.gov.tw/taiwan-website/5-gp/yearbook/chpt10-5.htm]. Rankings of economic freedom from The Heritage Foundation, *The Wall Street Journal*, Cato Institute, and the Fraser Institute. Starbucks information from Microsoft MSN. Asian company rankings from *Fortune* magazine's "Asia's Top 50" list, www.fortune.com August 2002. Anecdote on invention of Walkman from the book *Do You Remember Technology; Geeks, Gadgets + Gizmos?* (details in bibliography). Note on Chinese standard of living from University of Hawaii website [http://library.kcc.hawaii.edu/external/asdp/econ/Asian/barrett1.html].

Eight Signposts to Success

Eat the Elephant One Bite at a Time
Back ground information on Volkswagen drawn from *Getting the bugs out*, by David Kiley (details in bibliography).

Under promise and Over deliver

Credit *Far Eastern Economic Review* for NTT DoCoMo statistic. "Clan of the thumbs" and the "paka-paka girls" from *Technology Review: MIT's Magazine of Innovation*, April 2002, page 36; and *Asiaweek* October 12, 2001 respectively. Acer data source: *Far Eastern Economic Review*, May 24, 2001, www.feer.com. Comment from Sondhi Limthongkul from *Asiaweek* 1995 [http://www.Asiaweek.com/Asiaweek/95/1208/feat4.html].

Embrace Your Weaknesses

Chinese proverb quoted to Henry Kissinger by Lee Kuan Yew, found on Kissinger's website www.trilateral.org. Background on Tiger Balm from Interbrand [http://www.interbrand.com/features_profile.asp?id=12]. Red Bull section draws on references from Branding Asia [www.brandingasia.com].

The Vision Thing

Creative Technology information from the *Far Eastern Economic Review* [www.feer.com]. KFC in China: facts drawn from ACNielsen Media International (source: KFC company news release Oct 19, 2001) *Fast Company* magazine, August 2001 issue, and Piset Wattanavitukul, P.W. China Business Consultancy, Shanghai, PRC, in an e-newsletter posted on www.apmforum.com. Chunghwa background *Taipei Times,* October 8, 2001Move Upstream. The scholarly point of view on Korea that government "cleared roadblocks to corporate growth" is from *The Chaebol: Korea's New*

Industrial Might: Steers, Shin, and Ungson (details in bibliography). Ford brings LPG Falcon taxis to Hong Kong: Greenhouse Challenge [http://www.greenhouse.gov.au/challenge/html/achievements/success_stories/ford.html]. Statistics on the Hong Kong government move to LPG taxis from [www.cleartheair.org.hk].

Move Upstream

"Politicians are the culprits and businessmen are the accomplices," is a 1992 quote from Chung Ju Yung from the Korea Newspaper Editors Association.

Go, Go, Go!

Astra statistics from the *Far Eastern Economic Review* [http://www.feer.com/breaking_news/010523c.html]. Post-it note story from *How the Cadillac Got Its Fins* (details in bibliography). "Supercycle" product lifestyle information from *Wired* magazine [http://www.wired.com/wired/archive/9.09/topten_pr.html]. Sources on marketing and pricing numerology: *Price Endings in Asia:* Roger Heeler and Adma Nguyen, New York University [http://130.195.95.71:8081/WWW/ANZMAC2001/anzmac/AUTHORS/pdfs/Heeler.pdf]; and Chinese consumers' perception of alpha-numeric brand names: Swee Hoon Ang. *Journal of Consumer Marketing;* 14: 3 1997; pp. 220-233.

It's the Customer, Stupid

Customer must-do's: *Customers.com: How to Create A Profitable Business Strategy for the Internet & Beyond* by Patricia B. Seybold, and Ronni Marshak – contributor (details in bibliography). Lever Philippines bicycle distribution fact: *Fast Company*, May 2001. Amway India sachet-sized products: credit William Pinckney, managing director, Amway India [http://www.agencyfaqs.com/www1/news/interviews/pinckney.html]. Mercedes-Benz Taiwan information: source is Microsoft MSN.

Steal the Wheel

Background on Jollibee Foods from WorldBizWatch www.worldbizwatch.com. Background on lateral thinking from Edward de Bono's website http://www.edwdebono.com/debono/berry.htm. Samsung microwave oven story from *Fast Heat: How Korea Won the Microwave War:* Ira C. Magaziner and Mark Patinkin in the *Harvard Business Review* (details in bibliography).

Bibliography

Troubled Tiger: businessmen, bureaucrats, and generals in South Korea: Mark L. Clifford. An East Gate Book, by M.E. Sharpe, Inc. 1994. ISBN 1-56324-386-5

The Seven Habits of Highly Effective People: Powerful Lessons in Personal Change: Stephen R. Covey. Simon & Schuster Ltd London. 1989. ISN 0-671-71117-2

Do You Remember Technology; Geeks, Gadgets + Gizmos?: Michael Gitter, Sylvie Anapol, and Erika Glazer. Chronicle Books, San Francisco, The Do You Remember? Company, Inc. 2000.

Megatrends Asia: John Naisbitt. Touchstone Books, 1997. ISBN 0684827069

Permission Marketing: Turning Strangers Into Friends and Friends into Customers: Seth Godin. Simon & Schuster New York, NY. 1999. ISBN 0-684-85636-0

The Portable MBA in Marketing: Alexander Hiam and Charles D. Schewe. John Wiley & Sons, Inc. 1992. ISBN 0-471-54728-X

Marketing in South East Asia 2002: Market Survey Report. The second annual survey of marketing performance conducted by High-Tech Associates, in partnership with Ad Asia and The Chartered Institute of Marketing.

The Best Chinese Proverbs: compiled by Kai Hua. Hai Feng Publishing Co., Ltd. Hong Kong, 2000. ISBN 962-238-278-9

Getting the bugs out: the rise, fall and comeback of Volkswagen of America: David Kiley. John Wiley & Sons, Inc., New York. 2002 ISBN 0-471-40393-8

Lesly's Handbook of Public Relations and Communications, 4th Edition, edited by Philip Lesly. Probus Publishing Company, Chicago, IL 1991

The Cluetrain Manifesto; the End of Business as Usual: Rick Levine, Christopher Locke, Doc Searls, David Weinberger. Perseus Books, Cambridge Massachusetts. 2000. ISBN 0-7382-0244-4

The Marketing Imagination: Theodore Levitt. The Free Press; A Division of Macmillan, Inc., 1983, 1986. ISBN 0-02-919090-8

Fast Heat: How Korea Won the Microwave War: Ira C. Magaziner and Mark Patinkin in the Harvard Business Review 1988; *Harvard Consumer Strategies* reprint 89114.

How the Cadillac Got Its Fins and Other true Tales from the Annals of Business and Marketing: *Jack Mingo. HarperBusiness, Reprint edition June 1995. ASIN 0887307531*

Sons of the Yellow Emperor: Lynn Pan. Martin Secker & Warburg, 1990; Mandarin Paperback,s 1991. ISBN 0-7493-0860-5

Bottom Up Marketing: Al Ries & Jack Trout. McGraw Hill, 1989. ISBN 0-07-052733-4

The New Marketing Paradigm; Integrated Marketing Communications: Don E. Schultz, Stanley I. Tannenbaum; Robert F. Lauterborn. NTC Business Books, Division of NTC Publishing, Chicago, IL. 1994.
ISBN 0-8442-3452-4.

Emerging Chinese MNCs: Konka Group Company Limited: Professor Biswatosh Saha, Vinod Gupta School of Management at Indian Institute of Technology Kharagpur, India. The Asian Business Case Centre and AsiaCase.com, 2001.

Customers.com: How to Create A Profitable Business Strategy for the Internet & Beyond: Patricia B. Seybold, Ronni Marshak (Contributor) Times Books; 1 edition November 15, 1998. ISBN 0812930371

The Chaebol: Korea's New Industrial Might: Richard M. Steers, Yoo Keun Shin, Gerardo R. Ungson. Harper & Row, New York, NY. 1989.

Hi-Tech, Hi-Touch Branding: Creating Brand Power in the Age of Technology: Paul Temporal and KC Lee. John Wiley & Sons (Asia) Pte Ltd. ISBN 0-471-84596-5

Future Shock: Alvin Toffler. Bantam Books, Reissue edition 1991 (original edition 1970). ISBN 0553277375

Business Horizons, Relationship Marketing the Chinese Way. Oliver H.M. Yau, Issue: Jan, 2000

Media Asian Brands Poll 2002: leading brand exports making global headway; July 26, 2002

Index

G

H

I

J

U

V

W

X

Z